Leading from the Table

Leading from the Table

Paul Galbreath

THE
ALBAN
INSTITUTE
Herndon, Virginia
www.alban.org

The Alban Institute
2121 Cooperative Way, Suite 100
Herndon, VA 20171-5370

Unless otherwise noted, all Scripture quotations are from the New Revised Standard Version of the Bible, copyright © 1989, Division of Christian Education of the National Council of the Churches of Christ in the United States of America, and are used by permission.

Cover design by Tobias Becker, Bird Box Design.

Library of Congress Cataloging-in-Publication Data

Galbreath, Paul.
   Leading from the table / Paul Galbreath.
      p. cm.
   Includes bibliographical references.
   ISBN 978-1-56699-362-3
   1. Lord's Supper. 2. Christian leadership. I. Title.

BV825.3.G35 2008
264'.3—dc22
                                      2008004465

   12 11 10 09 08   VP   1 2 3 4 5

For Wes D. Lackey and John R. Fry
Mentors and Friends

Contents

Series Editor's Foreword

Healthy Congregations

Christianity is a "first-person plural" religion, where communal worship, service, fellowship, and learning are indispensable for grounding and forming individual faith. The strength of Christianity in North America depends on the presence of healthy, spiritually nourishing, well-functioning congregations. Congregations are the cradle of Christian faith, the communities in which children of all ages are supported, encouraged, and formed for lives of service. Congregations are the habitat in which the practices of the Christian life can flourish.

As living organisms, congregations are by definition in a constant state of change. Whether the changes are in membership, pastoral leadership, lay leadership, the needs of the community, or the broader culture, a crucial mark of healthy congregations is their ability to deal creatively and positively with change. The fast pace of change in contemporary culture, with its bias toward, not against, change only makes the challenge of negotiating change all the more pressing for congregations.

Vital Worship

At the center of many discussions about change in churches today is the topic of worship. This is not surprising, for worship is at the center of congregational life. To "go to church" means, for most members of congregations, "to go to worship." In *How Do*

We Worship? Mark Chaves begins his analysis with the simple assertion, "Worship is the most central and public activity engaged in by American religious congregations" (Alban Institute, 1999, p. 1). Worship styles are one of the most significant reasons that people choose to join a given congregation. Correspondingly, they are central to the identity of most congregations.

Worship is also central on a much deeper level. Worship is the locus of what several Christian traditions identify as the nourishing center of congregational life: preaching, common prayer, and the celebration of ordinances or sacraments. Significantly, what many traditions elevate to the status of "the means of grace" or even the "marks of the church" are essentially liturgical actions. Worship is central, most significantly, for theological reasons. Worship both reflects and shapes a community's faith. It expresses a congregation's view of God and enacts a congregation's relationship with God and each other.

We can identify several specific factors that contribute to spiritually vital worship and thereby strengthen congregational life.

- Congregations, and the leaders that serve them, need a shared vision for worship that is grounded in more than personal aesthetic tastes. This vision must draw on the deep theological resources of Scripture, the Christian tradition, and the unique history of the congregation.
- Congregational worship should be integrated with the whole life of the congregation. It can serve as the "source and summit" from which all the practices of the Christian life flow. Worship both reflects and shapes the life of the church in education, pastoral care, community service, fellowship, justice, hospitality, and every other aspect of church life.
- The best worship practices feature not only good worship "content," such as discerning sermons, honest prayers, creative artistic contributions, celebrative and meaningful rituals for baptism and the Lord's Supper. They also arise of out of good process, involving meaningful contributions from participants, thoughtful leadership, honest evaluation, and healthy communication among leaders.

Vital Worship, Healthy Congregations Series

The Vital Worship, Healthy Congregations Series is designed to reflect the kind of vibrant, creative energy and patient reflection that will promote worship that is both relevant and profound. It is designed to invite congregations to rediscover a common vision for worship, to sense how worship is related to all aspects of congregational life, and to imagine better ways of preparing both better "content" and better "process" related to the worship life of their own congregations.

It is important to note that strengthening congregational life through worship renewal is a delicate and challenging task precisely because of the uniqueness of each congregation. This book series is not designed to represent a single denomination, Christian tradition, or type of congregation. Nor is it designed to serve as arbiter of theological disputes about worship. Books in the series will note the significance of theological claims about worship, but they may, in fact, represent quite different theological visions from each other or from our work at the Calvin Institute of Christian Worship. That is, the series is designed to call attention to instructive examples of congregational life and to explore these examples in ways that allow readers in very different communities to compare and contrast these examples with their own practice. The models described in any given book may for some readers be instructive as examples to follow. For others, a given example may remind them of something they are already doing well or something they will choose not to follow because of theological commitments or community history.

Paul Galbreath's *Leading from the Table* offers a compelling reflection on the fundamental elements of a fulsome Lord's Supper celebration. Paul's reflections stand in the tradition of Ambrose and Augustine, who offered their most poignant reflections on the sacraments as reflections on actual practices, rather than as abstract treatises. This work also stands in the tradition of the prophets who lamented the disjunction between worship and ethics, liturgy and life in ancient Israel. Though Paul's words are more gentle than Amos or Isaiah, the insistence on integrity between worship and life is as crucial now as it was then, particularly in a land with significant resources. I heartily encourage readers to consider reading this book in conversation with others. If the Lord's Supper is fundamentally a communal act, and if the Christian life is fundamentally a set of community practices, then it follows naturally that healthy and robust reflection on both the Lord's Supper and a eucharistic way of life can best be cultivated together.

By promoting encounters with instructive examples from various parts of the body of Christ, we pray that these volumes will help leaders make good judgments about worship in their congregations and that, by the power of God's Spirit, these congregations will flourish.

John D. Witvliet
Calvin Institute of Christian Worship

Foreword

From the beginning, Christians gathered to worship God about a table. The first Christians were convinced that the risen Christ desired to offer the love of God in shared meals. So we read in the book of Acts that the early church continued in the teachings of the first witnesses, in mutual care, in the breaking of bread together, and in prayers for one another and for the world they were sent to serve. (Acts 2:42 paraphrased) The common life of those who wished to follow Jesus thus lead to and from the Lord's Table. This, of course, means that the liturgy—the pattern and actions of gathering to worship the mystery of God they experienced in, with, and through Jesus Christ—was focused at Christ's table. Yet it could never be confined to that table, for the living Christ was also to be found in everyday life's encounters.

What we read in Luke 24 where the journeying followers come to know him in the "breaking of the bread" finds its completion in Matthew 25 where the same Christ bids us serve all in need and thus meet and serve him. The Holy One whom we hear in the Word preached, prayed, and sung, and who feeds and heals us at the table, is the very one who will continue to reveal the grace of God when we serve others in Christ's name.

These truths are what undergird the illuminating pages that follow. This is the force of Paul Galbreath's chapters, beginning with the central reality that in learning to pray at the table we are learning to live. This life is the very gift God desires to lavish upon the world. This way of life is the very pattern we find outpoured in the life of the One who bids us welcome to the meal, and who blesses us on our way from the table. Each step of the way opens the wonder of how a meal can contain and compel us to embrace what God has embraced in creation and in redemption. Each step of the way also opens the wonder of what God has promised the whole world in prophecy, covenant and eschatological hope.

Perhaps we could put a major point of this book in the following image: Holy Communion (the Lord's Supper, the Eucharist) invites us to a double journey. This Christ-meal invites us to enter deeply into the mystery of God's grace and simultaneously invites us to enter deeply into our own humanity. And like a true feast itself, we cannot enjoy the nourishment and the delight without also being with the host and with others around the table. But this feasting also brings deep awareness of gratitude for and mutuality with both host and fellow guests.

This "double journey" of faith, then, requires that we learn how to commune with host and one another but also how to live out of the nourishment and gratitude that has been given with the feast. This is made clear again and again in early testimonies, such as found in Justin Martyr's mid-second-century writings. He refers to how the Eucharist cannot simply be contained within the four walls of the meeting place but must be taken out and distributed to those not present. Moreover, the gifts that the community offers in response to the invitation are themselves given to take care of "orphans and widows, and those who are in want on account of sickness or any other cause, and those who are in bonds, and the strangers who are sojourners." This sounds precisely like an extension of what we read in relevant New Testament passages. Theology of the sacrament of the Holy Meal cannot be divorced from the ethics of service. This is, of course, the very heartbeat of this book.

At the same time this is a very practical "pastoral" book. It is addressed to both those who lead congregations and to all who are in the Christian assembly—the entire "laity" as we say. Those who lead by reading, praying, leading congregational song, as well as those who preside at the table, are "prompters" of the liturgy of the gathered congregation. Likewise, those who are in the pews are also responsible and accountable to the Word and the Table. Three of the worst heresies of our times can be summed up this way: 1) when worship is done for the assembly; 2) when worship is projected at the assembly—as high-powered entertainment, for

example; and 3) when the assembly comes unprepared and un-
ready to participate deeply and honestly. This book should make
clear that both those who lead and those who respond do the liturgy together.

In this way hospitality is a liturgical action, as is offering ourselves, as is praying for others and the whole world. All this is not
a "one-time" thing. Rather, the journey to and from the table of
Jesus Christ takes time. Furthermore, it is always over time and
in time (human history and real circumstances) that the reality of
what we do at the Lord's Table is revealed to us and to the world.
This is why we must call it both a mystery and something we must
do together. As the author makes clear in chapters 4 and 5, it is a
matter of our very identity as the people of God and our way of
life.

I happily commend this book for congregational study. It certainly should find its way into every pastor's study (in both senses
of that word). It would be revelatory to a congregation should it be
used as a course of study for the Session, the adult Sunday school
classes, and the baptismal and confirmation classes. It is written in
light of the generous liturgical resources available to Presbyterians
by way of the Book of Common Worship, the Hymnal and other
texts. I think it is also a deeply ecumenical book, and I would
hope that it might bring churches of different denominations together around its profound subject matter.

> Don E. Saliers, Wm. R. Cannon Distinguished
> Professor of Theology and Worship Emeritus,
> Candler School of Theology, Emory University

Preface

This book began around a table in a bar on the fifteenth floor of a hotel in New Haven, Connecticut. There my friend Craig Satterlee persuaded me to send a proposal to the Alban/Calvin Institute for Christian Worship (CICW) editorial board for a book outlining my interest in the ethical shape of ways that we gather and pray around the communion table. What had started out as a fairly straightforward project quickly grew in complexity as I thought about the differences in communion practice in vastly different denominations and congregations. Despite the difficulties and distinctions, I still believe that there is value to be gained by reflecting together from different Christian perspectives about an ecumenical pattern for prayer at the table and the consequences of the ways in which we live out this prayer. In this endeavor I need to ask the reader's indulgence to overlook areas that may not apply to present practice in your own context.

At the same time, it is important for me to be open about my own context and identity. I write as a Presbyterian minister who served in parish ministry for ten years, for three years as a denominational officer in the Office of Theology and Worship of the Presbyterian Church (U.S.A.), and in the past few years as a worship professor at Union Theological Seminary and Presbyterian School of Christian Education, in Richmond, Virginia. These opportunities for service in the church have shaped and nurtured my understanding of worship and in particular of the sacrament of communion. While I have sought out and learned from a wide variety of congregations and ecumenical contexts, I nevertheless bring my primary identity as a Reformed theologian to the topic of this book. I do not attempt to disguise these commitments but hope that readers will find parallels to their own settings that will allow them to discover helpful insights and connections.

Several significant factors made this project possible. First, I am grateful to the Alban/CICW editorial board for endorsing an undertaking of this kind. In particular, I express my deep appreciation to Beth Gaede, who is an incredibly supportive, reliable, and helpful editor. I am especially grateful to the Wabash Center in Crawfordsville, Indiana, for providing a grant that allowed me writing time to complete this manuscript. The initial impetus to work in this direction began while I was serving in the Office of Theology and Worship. Joe Small, my supervisor, gave me time, space, and encouragement to begin my initial explorations into the relationship between sacraments and ethical actions. My colleagues in that work listened carefully to early reflections on the relationship between worship and mission. In that setting, the Calvin Institute provided a generous grant that enabled conversations with pastors and church leaders as well as work with pilot churches. Steve Shussett was a part of those conversations, and I am thankful for his continued friendship and for his contribution to this project by preparing the discussion questions at the end of each chapter. Special thanks as well to colleagues and students at Union-PSCE whose encouragement and insights prompted this work.

Members of congregations where I served as pastor will recognize themselves in many of the stories told in these pages. I am grateful for the opportunities to learn and teach with people in churches in Clatskanie, Woodburn, and Warrenton, Oregon, where I served as an interim pastor. Special thanks are due to the members of Immanuel Presbyterian Church in Tacoma, Washington, where I was pastor for six wonderful and challenging years. These opportunities to ground community life around the common experiences of worship continue to nurture and inform my faith.

This book is dedicated to two long-term mentors, Wes Lackey and John Fry. Wes taught me to love liturgy and instilled in me a passion for pursuing its effect on the lives of congregations. John challenged me to press relentlessly for the ethical actions and outcomes of those who gather in worship. While I am sure that they will not agree with all of the conclusions that I have reached, I hope that they will recognize their influence in the questions that I raise and in the direction that I head. I am fortunate to have them as mentors and particularly blessed to count them as friends. I have also been aided by colleagues who read drafts of the manuscript and offered helpful correctives, questions, and insights. My thanks go especially to Gordon Lathrop, Janet Walton, and Cláudio Carvalhaes, who provided helpful commentary and gracious encouragement.

This work would not have been possible without the constant love and support of my wife, Jan. Much that I have learned about hospitality and grace comes from her. In addition, she read early drafts of the manuscript and offered valuable corrections. In other significant ways, our son Andy is a conversation partner who constantly prods me to think more carefully and clearly about the claims and presuppositions of liturgical language. My life, work, and faith are deeply enriched by their presence in my life.

Finally, I offer this modest work toward the ongoing transformation of the work and witness of the church. It is my deep hope and belief that when congregations are grounded in word, water, bread, and wine, then the transformative power of God's Spirit has room to work among us. When we hear and discover our identity in the Word that is read and proclaimed, when we are named as disciples of Jesus Christ, when we grow in faithfulness in the waters of baptism that claim us as children of God, and when we live in the spirit of hospitality around a table where bread is broken and wine is shared in thanksgiving for God's goodness, then we are blessed with a community that will sustain us to work for justice and peace in this world.

CHAPTER 1

Coming to the Table

The minister moved slowly from the pulpit to the table. It was Christmas Eve, and the church was filled with families with happy, eager children awaiting the Christmas celebration. Even as he shared their joy, the pastor carried sad news to impart to the congregation. Earlier that day, Bob, the beloved patriarch of the congregation, had died unexpectedly. Just two weeks ago, Bob had stood at the front of the church and had sung in the choir's seasonal music celebration. And now he was gone. The pastor knew many in the congregation had not yet heard of Bob's death. It was his responsibility to share the news. He decided to wait until he came to the table to celebrate communion.

He took a deep breath and, with a catch in his voice and tears in his eyes, he announced: "This morning, Bob Arpke, our friend and brother in Christ, passed away. As we gather at this table, we celebrate this communion in memory and thanksgiving for his life." The minister worried that visitors to the church would be put off by the emotional outpouring of the occasion. At this happy, festive Christmas Eve celebration, he was acutely aware that he had inserted other emotions into the gathering. And yet, what else could he do? Only at communion, as the church family gathered around the table, did he believe that he could do justice to sharing the joy and sorrow of the life of the congregation. Amid tears of loss and the joy of the birth of the Christ child, the congregation shared once again in the movement of God's grace and good news in our world.

At the communion table, our prayer finds a shape and form that guide our thoughts and actions. There we discover ourselves in the story of God's faithfulness in creating, sustaining, and nurturing us as a community of faith and as individuals. In this place there is room for praise and thanksgiving, for supplication and lamentation. We gather at the table with food and drink, and we come to be close to each other; we are surrounded by food and drink and the presence of one another. There, by the very presence of one story, one prayer, one bread, one cup, and the one Spirit, we find our lives woven together.

And so on this Christmas Eve, the people joined together to give thanks for God's faithful presence through creation, in Christ, and in the Spirit who enlivens us. They gave thanks for those who had lived beside them as witnesses and even saints. This communion prayer served as a container for the story of God's grace and for the discovery of their identity as children of God. They prayed with tears as they expressed their sense of loss. They prayed with hope for their friend's family and for their comfort in this time of grief. They prayed with gratitude that their lives had been woven together and that all had shared this meal many times before.

No place other than the table provides this opportunity. The table stands as an intersection between Word and Sacrament, between memory and hope, between pastor and congregation, between receiving and serving, and between community and individual. Leading from the table is a way of thinking, speaking, acting, and living that grows out of learning to recognize and embody these connections in our lives as a congregation and as individuals.

Changing Times

Congregations from a wide variety of denominations have undergone great change in worship practices during the past fifty years. Among the most dramatic changes has been the increase in the frequency of communion. The quarterly norm for communion celebration in some Protestant church bodies is rapidly fading in favor of at least a monthly gathering. Much of the impetus for this movement has come about through ecumenical cooperation. The dramatic changes of Vatican II in the Roman Catholic Church in the 1960s served as an impetus in many Protestant congregations to reexamine worship practices. At the center of this investigation was a reexamination of the role and place of communion in the life of congregations. The work of liturgical renewal was advanced by two major factors:

1. *An increased sense of ecumenical cooperation among denominations and congregations*: To cite one example of the growing sense of partnership between communions, the publication of *Baptism, Eucharist and Ministry*[1] elucidated shared understandings of worship patterns and practices while noting the continued differences and distinctions that remained. (Still, the inability to reconcile distinctive understandings about communion remains a major impediment to full ecumenical cooperation within the body of Christ.)

2. *A reexamination of the historical and theological framework of denominational identity*: By the end of the twentieth century, many Episcopalians and Lutherans reclaimed weekly gathering at the table as part of the standard of the Lord's Day service. Presbyterians began to rearticulate John Calvin's vision of the unification of Word and Sacrament as normative. Even amid ongoing strife and division around matters of worship style, the movement toward increasing communion frequency continues to grow. In recent years, the emergent church movement, with its emphasis on recovering ancient worship practices for younger generations, has served as a catalyst in pressing for weekly communion.

Examination of the shape and significance of the prayer at the communion table as a pattern for our daily lives as a community and as individuals seeks to build on and to extend the work of both of these movements. We are fortunate to have inherited the work of those within the ecumenical movement who have helped us recognize the importance of our unity as brothers and sisters in Christ. At the same time, turning our attention toward the shape of the table prayer may point to a way to overcome problems between factions in the church that have difficulty recognizing shared practices. Gathering around the table can prompt congregations to

explore ways of building partnerships with other local congregations. To put it another way, fellowship at table around shared
meals can deepen friendships between groups of Christians who,
while continuing to hold distinct theological perspectives (including different theological understandings of what happens at communion), may find their lives connected and woven together by
shared practices. In this age of post-Christendom, the shared witness of Christian assemblies is desperately needed to provide ways
for those outside the Christian faith to make sense of the odd divisions that we have created within the church.

The current division between traditional and contemporary
worship styles often serves to foster division within congregations
by highlighting demographic and consumer patterns as the primary labels of our Christian identity. Giving renewed emphasis to
table practices and connecting the shape of the communion prayer
with the patterns of our lives provide a way to unite us rather than
to separate us into interest groups.

Developing leadership skills that connect the congregation's
table practice to the life and work of the church is essential to
moving toward unity. While developing leadership does include
strengthening presiding skills, this book is not a how-to manual
on presiding techniques. Readers can find material from their own
traditions to address this need. Rather, this book is a series of reflections about the way the prayer at the communion table provides a pattern for our lives and our actions. This work presents
an analysis of communion prayers in order to relate them to the
broader life of the congregation. The goal is to shift our understanding of table prayer from a formula led by the pastor to a road
map that highlights intersections between the practices at the table
and the daily practices in the life of the community that gathers
around the table.

Praying at the Table: Back to the Basics

In one of the oldest descriptions of Christian worship that dates
back to the second century, early Christian apologist Justin Martyr described the practices of those who gathered on Sunday. The

service included the reading of Scripture from the apostles or the prophets and a sermon that encouraged listeners to follow these biblical patterns and examples. Then the assembly gathered for communion.

> Then we stand up together and offer prayers. And, as we mentioned before, when we have finished the prayer, bread is presented, and wine with water; the president likewise offers up prayers and thanksgiving according to his ability, and the people assent by saying Amen.[2]

There are a couple of important things to notice in this brief summary. First, everyone is involved in the act and posture of communion prayer. The community stands and prays together. Clear and effective presiding prompts everyone to participate in giving thanks to God for calling us together as a community of faith. Second, the presider's gift of leading the community in prayer is acknowledged with the peculiar words that prayer is offered "according to his ability." For me, the immediate image that comes to mind is that of a gracious host at a dinner party. We all have experienced the tone that is set as we participate in gatherings led by friends, colleagues, and acquaintances. The host's gifts of hospitality establish the tone of the gathering. Whether it is the host's enthusiastic welcome, attention to detail, or sense of delight in calling people together, the host's gifts create a unique setting. While the words may often be the same ("We are so glad you could come this evening!"), we all have experienced that it is not just what is said to welcome us but how it is said that makes all the difference.

An additional and essential element appears in Justin Martyr's ancient report of the church gathered around the table. Justin finished his description:

> The elements which have been "eucharistized" are distributed and received by each one; and they are sent to the absent by the deacons. Those who are prosperous, if they wish, contribute what each one deems appropriate; and the collection is deposited with the president; and he takes care of the orphans and widows, and those who are needy because of sickness or other

cause, and the captives, and the strangers who sojourn amongst us—in brief, he is the curate of all who are in need.[3]

It is remarkable that in a brief description of Christian gathering, Justin spends so much time talking about the importance of linking the food at the table with the action of providing for the hungry. It is a sign that the early church avoided the distinctions that we often make today between worship and mission. There was no separation into committee structures and interest groups. Instead, the central act of gathering around the table was the foundation for providing food for those who otherwise would go hungry. Widows, prisoners, and the sick, who outside of relatives had few if any resources, were fed by the offerings from the table. More than just a bit of bread and sip of wine, the meal at the table was an occasion to feed those who gathered around it and those who couldn't come but whose well-being depended on the further distribution of the table's food.

In the coming chapters, we will keep these two basic themes from Justin Martyr at the center of our conversation. First, we will note how the table prayer leads to the whole congregation's involvement in the work of the church. Second, we will pay particular attention to the way that actions at the table lead to the mission and outreach of the church. The goal is to reconnect with Justin's vision of the table, collecting our prayers and connecting us with the needs of those around us.

Praying at the Table

Denominational distinctions may place different emphases on how prayers at the communion table are offered. In some traditions, a specific text from a prayer book is required or expected. Other traditions value a sense of freedom and extemporaneous qualities in the prayer at the table. While the practices may vary, ecumenical discussions and agreements can help us identify certain basic shared patterns.

The prayer at table is *trinitarian.* Coming to the table is a way to continually renew our baptismal identity. In baptism, we are baptized by water and the Spirit in the name of God, the Father, Son, and Holy Spirit, and welcomed as sons and daughters of God and brothers and sisters in Jesus Christ. This God is known to us in the beauty of the world around us and in the history of those who have gone before us. This God is known to us in the particular expression of Jesus Christ, whose life, death, and resurrection serve as the primary witness to God's presence among us. And this God is known to us in the work of the Spirit, who opens our ears and hearts to hear God's word, connects us to one another, and prompts and calls us to faithful living. Our identity grows out of the trinitarian language of the prayer offered by those who gather around the table. While communion prayers in worship books and in free traditions may use different language, they share a commonality in giving thanks to the God whom we know as three-in-one.

The prayer at table is *biblical.* Scripture provides patterns that guide and direct our worship. Much of the language of communion prayers grows out of biblical texts and images from Scripture. Throughout this study, we will look to biblical patterns that undergird the shape of prayer at table and provide a sense of direction for our lives.

The prayer at table is *a story.* At the table our prayer tells the story of God's love of the world, God's incarnation in Jesus Christ, and God's presence in the Spirit. It is a story that is shared by all those who gather around the table to break bread and share the cup.

The prayer at table is *communal.* It is not just the presider's private prayer but is first and foremost the prayer of all those who gather at the table. Common responses provide ways to include other voices. The prayer and actions around the table seek also to create community. By its very nature, the action of sharing one loaf of bread and sharing a common cup are dramatic enactments of the communal claims on our lives. This is not a private meal but a shared event that brings people together.

The prayer at table is also *physical.* Although a great deal of helpful literature has been written about the spiritual aspects and benefits of communion, this basic characteristic is often overlooked. The one presiding embodies the prayer at the table. Through gesture we are welcomed to come and eat. In some traditions, the act of coming forward is a way of physically responding to the invitation to the table. Receiving the communion elements may include kneeling, extending one's hands, eating and drinking, and making the sign of the cross on one's body. In other traditions, the elements may be brought to the assembly and passed through the pews. In this instance, the act of serving one's neighbor, receiving the elements, eating, and drinking are physical responses to the invitation to the table.

Finally, the prayer at table is characterized by a sense of *expectancy.* We hope and believe that the community gathered around the table will experience the presence of the risen Christ in the breaking of the bread and the sharing of the cup. Likewise, we gather at the table with a sense of expectation that this event will change and transform us. We share bread and wine with those whom we love and with whom we agree and also those with whom we differ. We share communion with friends and with strangers. These practices alone can help us expand our understanding of Christian fellowship. As we will note later, we do not gather alone at the table but in solidarity with all of the faithful of every time and place in hope as we look to the day when all will gather at the Lord's table.

Leadership Traits at the Table

Bringing to life the various characteristics of prayer around the table requires strong leadership skills. Since the table prayer itself requires a sense of expectation, leaders need to cultivate a sense of expectation that something is going to happen when they invite the community to gather at the table. A dull and dreary reading of a prayer text from a worship book or a hurried rush through the Words of Institution to get the congregation out of worship on time does little to create a sense of encounter, engagement, and transformation within the congregation. In my own tradition, while liturgical renewal has led to a significant increase in the frequency of communion, far too often the practice itself remains locked in the older pattern of mournful, private introspection rather than a hopeful, transformative encounter with the presence of Christ in the breaking of the bread. Congregational renewal is catalyzed by leaders who expect and articulate Christ's presence in our lives (both in times of loss and in times of joy). Effective leaders convey an attitude of hope and trust in God's faithfulness as they welcome all to the table.

Leadership at the table requires a sense of *transparency*. Prayers at the table reveal the presider's gifts and expectations. The uniqueness of voice, intonation, and gesture makes prayers sound and feel distinctive. Effective leaders learn to use their gifts in ways that point beyond themselves to the presence of God. It is important to note here that leadership skills are connected to personality traits. Congregations respond to the ways they hear and see the Word present in their leaders' lives. Awareness of one's personality traits allows a leader to use his or her gifts in service of creating space for the Spirit's work as we gather at the table. At the same time, leaders must be careful that the prayer at table does not become a colloquial expression that simply reinforces their own sense of self.

Perhaps the most basic leadership skill is a sense of *presence*. Effective leadership at the table is characterized by a pervasive and persuasive sense that something significant is happening as the community gathers around the table. People in the pews have an innate ability to identify the genuine beliefs of their leaders. When leadership is grounded in a conviction of the centrality of the table, congregations will also recognize its importance. It is worth noting that visitors in the congregation can usually recognize immediately what stands at the center of a congregation's identity. Often visitors can do so more clearly and quickly than longtime members of a congregation whose history of involvement and personal investment may color their perspectives. A leader's strong sense of presence at the table enhances the congregation's ability to experience the gift of Christ in the breaking of bread and the sharing of the cup.

Leadership at the table grows out of a sense of *embodiment*. While handbooks provide guidance about appropriate gestures, this skill involves more than following a manual. It entails learning to take the prayer into one's body and to offer it up as a gift that invites the congregation to join in the prayer. For some, the written words of a table prayer are spoken in ways that give the words new implications and accents. Emphasizing particular phrases can break open familiar prayers and lead to new understandings. For example, a Korean pastor offering the invitation to the table after a sermon on the division of Korean people and the call for unity in Christ emphasizes that the invitation to the table is to *people who come from north and south* (and repeats these words a second time). The words resonate deeply and have a significant impact. In other settings, a free prayer in the presider's own words still follows the shape and contour of historical and ecumenical communion prayers. In both instances, presiders point to theological claims in the prayer by the way the prayer is embodied in physical posture and the sound of the voice.

Leading at the table grows out of the distinctive *narrative* dimensions of the prayer. A sense of drama and movement permeates the prayer. It is a form of embodied storytelling that includes gestures that undergird and support the story of God's redemptive work in our world. Leaders learn to cultivate the narrative quality of this prayer by paying careful attention to the dramatic movements within the structure of the prayer. Seasonal variation throughout the church year provides different moods that color the telling of the story. A celebration of communion on Palm/Passion Sunday or Maundy Thursday will likely point to the tragic dimension of Christ's journey to the cross, whereas the Easter Sunday celebration is filled with images of resurrection and new life. I like to speak about the communion prayer as a prayer with our eyes open, in which the presider engages the congregation in the retelling of the story of God's presence in our past, present, and future.

Finally, leadership at the table that makes a lasting impression grows out of a conviction that the prayer at table provides a *pattern* for our lives. This pattern begins with the presider who understands that coming to the table is foundational to his or her ministry and service. This basic conviction allows the prayer to avoid becoming routine or a matter of simply going through the

motions. Healthy congregations centered in worship recognize
that the patterns of prayer around the table are patterns that will ✓
support their work and service in the world.

Language, Life, and Christian Identity

Denominational traditions vary in the language used to speak
of communion. *Eucharist* (which means thanksgiving) is used in
some settings. Others refer to the table as the *Lord's Supper. Communion, Holy Communion,* and *Mass* are other ways of speaking
about this event. While the language may vary, these traditions
all recognize the same event as a sacrament, a sign of God's presence. Although distinctions in language, theology, and practice
remain an obstacle to the hope of the church's sharing one meal
that shows its unity, the fact that Christians share similar versions
of this meal at all is an astounding testimony to the centrality of
the table. The rapid expansion of the early church into widely differing cultural contexts did not diminish the basic understanding
that the table stands at the center of Christian identity. Historical evidence continues to show that while communion practices
varied greatly in the early years of the church (and included different elements), the centrality of the meal has remained constant
throughout the history of the church. While Reformers questioned
and critiqued theological assumptions and understandings, they
did not dispute the significance of communion. Both Martin Luther and John Calvin called for changes in communion practices
that would renew the congregation's role and participation. At the
center of these changes was agreement on the importance of the
assembly's involvement in the practices of praying and coming to
the table. An increase in communion frequency, while less than
hoped for by some reformers (Calvin and Luther both argued for
communion as part of each Lord's Day gathering), was nevertheless significant.

This book uses the language of table prayer and practice as a
basic category, while at times using other words as synonyms. As
a common shape for the table prayer, we will follow an outline
found in one worship book (see box on page 12). This summary

The outline below is provided to guide those who desire to pray the great thanksgiving in a free style.

The prayer begins with thankful praise to God

> For God's work in creation and providence, and in covenant history;
> For the witness of the prophets;
> For God's steadfast love in spite of human failure;
> For the ultimate gift of Christ;
> And for the immediate occasion or festival.

The prayer continues with thankful recalling of the acts of salvation in Jesus Christ:

> Redemption;
> Christ's birth, life, and ministry;
> Christ's death and resurrection;
> His present intercession for us and the promise of his coming again;
> The gift of the Sacrament.

The Holy Spirit is called upon

> To lift all who share in the feast into Christ's presence;
> To make the breaking of the bread and sharing of the cup a participation in the body and blood of Christ;
> To make us one with the risen Christ and with all God's people;
> To unite us in communion with all the faithful in heaven and earth;
> To nourish us with the body of Christ so that we may mature into the fullness of Christ;
> To keep us faithful as Christ's body, representing Christ in ministry in the world,
> In anticipation of the fulfillment of the kingdom Christ proclaimed.

There follows an ascription of praise to the triune God.[4]

shows the patterns and categories of table prayers that are accept-
ed and used in a wide variety of Christian traditions.

Each chapter in this book provides an outline of a part of the
communion prayer and points to ways that the prayer connects
to the work and witness of the congregation's life. Effective leaders work to articulate and draw out the connections between the
movements of the prayer around the table and the congregation's
understanding of and commitment to serving as disciples of Jesus
Christ. By exploring this trajectory, we seek to show how ethical
practices that grow out of coming to the table can serve as a way
to recognize the unity of the church that holds Word and Table at
the center of its life.

Congregational Renewal around the Table:
A Brief Testimony

The new pastor entered the chapel for the Thursday evening weekly communion service during the season of Lent. Only two members of the congregation were sitting in the front pews awaiting
his arrival. The brief, simple service of Word and Table was new
for the congregation, which until recently had celebrated communion only four times each year. But the new pastor was committed
to the work of congregational redevelopment that grew out of a
worship-centered congregational identity. He realized that sharing
weekly communion strengthened him and others to continue the
hard work of redevelopment in this congregation.

At the first meeting of the session (congregational governing
board) following Easter, the elders of the church reviewed the services. While supportive of the increased number of services in the
Holy Week schedule, one elder inquired about attendance at the
weekly communion service. The pastor reported the sparse turn-
out, and a lengthy discussion ensued. Some of the church leaders suggested that the additional service was an ineffective use
of the pastor's time because of its limited impact on the congregation. The pastor decided that at this point it would be unwise
to force the issue by defending the service. This group needed to
sort through this matter itself. At last, a younger member of the

session spoke up. "In my business," she reported, "we do not make decisions after trying something one time. Instead, we try things for about three years to determine if they will have a lasting impression." Quickly a consensus emerged that if the pastor did not object to leading these services, maybe a future for these services would emerge.

In the coming years, slowly but surely the Thursday evening Lenten services grew. And with them, members of the congregation deepened their sense of community with one another. As members participated regularly, the prayer at the table gradually became their prayer. Sunday worship services were shaped by those whose experiences in the Lenten services (and at other special midweek communion celebrations on feast days) brought a new depth of commitment, which carried the congregation into its work of rebuilding and renewing the congregation's life. Even the major Christmas and Easter Sunday celebrations were undergirded by the regular members in the congregation rather than being a strange event for friends and visitors of the congregation to observe passively. Over the course of years, a new identity emerged in the congregation. The transition was not without question, struggle, or opposition. However, a steadfast commitment to *the central act of gathering regularly around the table* provided a foundation for congregational renewal. In a congregation that continued to experience the deaths of significant numbers of long-term members, the experiences of sorrow and joy found their expression around the meeting place at the communion table. Through times of difficult transition, gathering around the table provided a source of comfort and hope.

These changes did not come overnight. No magic programs or quick fixes are proposed here. Instead, congregational leadership centered at the table takes a deliberate, long-term commitment to restore, build upon, and nurture the foundational element of the congregation as it gathers regularly in prayer around the table. In the following chapters, we will explore the biblical and ethical components that are a part of the church's prayer as it gathers around the table. Paying attention to the basic patterns of prayer at the table and exploring the implications and consequences for the church's mission will point to opportunities for growth and renewal in congregational life and identity.

Only at the table, where all are welcome, where bread is broken and wine is poured, where voices are raised in prayer and supplication, can we find a common place that orients us as we move through times of change and turmoil by uniting us with witnesses from the past who point us towards a new future.

Hymn for Reflection

Down to earth, as a dove,
Came to light holy love:
Jesus Christ from above
Bringing great salvation
Meant for every nation.
Let us sing, sing, sing,
Dance and spring, spring, spring,
Christ is here,
Ever near!
Gloria in excelsis.

This is love come to light,
Now is fear put to flight.
God defeats darkest night,
Giving for our sorrows
Hope of new tomorrows.
Let us sing, sing, sing,
Dance and spring, spring, spring,
Christ is here,
Ever near!
Gloria in excelsis.

Christ the Lord comes to feed
Hungry people in need;
In the house there is bread:
Jesus in a stable,
In the church a table.

Let us sing, sing, sing,
Dance and spring, spring, spring,
Christ is here,
Ever near!
Gloria in excelsis.[5]

Questions for Discussion

1. Some communion liturgies begin with the words, "This is the joyful feast of the people of God." Does this describe the "celebration" of the Lord's Supper in your church's life, or is the service mournful in its expression? Think about the music you hear in connection with communion: does it express Maundy Thursday or Easter? Consider the juxtaposition of rejoicing with those who rejoice on a merry Christmas and mourning with those who mourn. Have you attended a service witnessing to the resurrection (more commonly known as a funeral) in which the Lord's Supper was celebrated? In what ways is this an appropriate response of the faithful?

2. Consider your own dinner table. How often do you eat with loved ones and friends? Can it ever be too often? How are conversations begun and differences of opinion expressed? How are joys shared and problems discussed? And what does the way we eat at "our" table say about the Lord's Table?

3. Do you see a relationship between "the food at the table" and "providing for the hungry"? If so, what is it? How do you see the effect of this relationship in your church and in your life? Is there a connection between mission and outreach and the Table? If so, what is it?

4. It is not unusual for someone who is sick or grieving to receive gifts of food from others. Is there a connection between these gifts and "the gifts of God for the people of God"?

5. Recite or sing together the Hymn for Reflection on pages 15–16. How do these words reflect on the chapter you have just read or the conversation you have shared? Consider in particular the final stanza and the words:

Christ the Lord comes to feed
Hungry people in need;
In the house there is bread:
Jesus in a stable,
In the church a table.

6. What are the relationships between hungry people and bread in our houses? Or between Jesus's birth in a stable and the table within the church?

CHAPTER 2

Gathering around the Table

A line of homeless people gathers on the sidewalk just outside the building of a downtown church. Throughout the cold morning, the line lengthens in anticipation of a free meal in the Stew Pot—the soup kitchen that the church hosts. My colleague and I walk outside to meet people who are waiting in line just as an old station wagon pulls up. Robert, who is driving the car, is bringing boxes of clothes, sweaters, and blankets to hand out. Rapidly, the people descend upon the car and snatch up the clothing that will keep them warm during the winter. Once the clothes are distributed, Robert sees that we are visitors, walks over, and begins to talk with us.

We ask him how he got started handing out clothes. "In the past," he says, "I figure I was a Christian about two hours each week—when I went to church services. By serving the homeless, I figure I am living like a Christian about twenty hours a week!" He offers a wry and candid assessment of the way many of us have been led to think about Christian faith. For many, the time we spend in the church building is the designated time for us to be Christian. Then it is back to the real world, where so often the language of the church remains foreign and abstract. But for Robert, meeting and working with homeless people is one way to practice the claims of Scripture. As he hands out clothes, he learns to look for the presence of Christ in neighbors and strangers.

Robert looks at his station wagon and the street people who still surround it and says to us: "This is communion." This gathering, this welcoming of strangers, this distribution of the elements, these actions have seeped into Robert's life and thoughts in a way

that makes the parallels between service and communion so striking that he sees and articulates them as all part of the same act.

His observation surprises us. For him, serving communion
happens not only at table in church, but also as he works on the
street with homeless people. He has transferred the reception of
bread and wine from inside the church to serving those outside
the walls of the church. This act of feeding the hungry, and clothing those without resources, regardless of the reason, helps him
recognize the presence of Christ in the broken lives and broken
world around him. He started breaking bread and sharing the cup
around the table, but now his vision has expanded.

Robert sees his service collecting and distributing clothes to
street people in light of his experience at the table. When congregational renewal is centered on the table, artificial separations
between worship and mission no longer make sense. These actions
blend together. Effective church leaders connect these practices by
pointing to the fullness of Christian life. Even as the separation
between sacred and secular has been called into question by many
(for in God's hands, all time is sacred time), so too worship cannot
be confined to the brief times we gather inside church buildings.
The events and experiences at the table become overlaid on other
times and places in our lives.

In this chapter we look to Scripture to identify connections
between Holy Communion and Christian service. Uncovering basic Christian meal patterns that emerged from the very beginning
of the church is a primary way we can assess our own practices.
This struggle to connect worship and mission is not just a by-
product of the twenty-first-century age of specialization; it has
been a part of the ongoing struggle of the church to assert that
Christian discipleship is a recognition of and response to God's
claim on all parts of our lives.

The Ethics of Eating

A congregation gathered in the common meeting area for its
weekly communion service. Each group brought food and wine to

the celebration. Some were able to get to the service early and set up places to eat. They saved room for their friends to join them around their makeshift tables. Others in the church community had to work longer hours and arrived late to the gathering. With little time and limited resources to prepare a meal, the latecomers found themselves sitting at the back of the room, watching as others ate rich food and drank good wine.

Over time, the gathering became rowdy. Those who had brought generous portions of food consumed it. Some became drunk, while others did not even have enough to eat. The divisions between the haves and the have-nots were reinforced by the eating practices centered on the community's table fellowship.

If this description of worship and community practices sounds disturbing yet vaguely familiar, it is because the description comes from the apostle Paul's first letter to the church in Corinth. This earliest written description of communion practices from 1 Corinthians includes a blistering critique of the practices in the congregation. After reviewing the reports he has received about the gathering, Paul concludes with these words: "When you come together, it is not really to eat the Lord's Supper" (1 Cor. 11:20). Or to put it another way: You may have thought that you were gathering for communion, but these practices are contrary to what it means to celebrate the Lord's Supper.

First, Paul proceeds to offer ethical advice. He tells the church in Corinth: you need to examine your eating habits. It is not right for some to have plenty to eat and drink (perhaps even too much!) while others go hungry. Gathering around the table should lead to equitable distribution. Healthy table practices promote the healing of divisions in congregations, rather than reinforcing patterns that separate and isolate.

Immediately following this admonition, Paul reminds the congregation that the primary pattern for gathering at the table draws from the life and teaching of Jesus. Our tradition and reason for coming to the table reflect on the example of Christ, who gathered the disciples together in the upper room, where they shared the bread and the cup. Continuing this basic practice, Paul asserts, is a form of proclamation of the gospel.

For the proclamation to be enacted, though, the community must heed Paul's word of warning: "Whoever, therefore, eats the bread or drinks the cup of the Lord in an unworthy manner will be answerable for the body and blood of the Lord. Examine yourselves, and only then eat of the bread and drink of the cup" (1 Cor. 11:27-28). This text has often been used as a warrant for private introspection about one's own spiritual condition to determine whether one feels worthy to receive the communion elements. In the context of Paul's discussion of communion malpractice in the Corinthian congregation, such an interpretation is misguided! The issue for Paul is not about trying to determine our worthiness to participate. If this were the case, then by Paul's own theological analysis, none of us would be worthy to receive communion. (Think, for instance, of Paul's assessment of the human condition in Romans 1–3, which concludes with these well-known words: "since all have sinned and fall short of the glory of God" [Rom. 3:23].) Instead, Paul's attention is focused on the external practices of eating and drinking in equitable ways with those gathered around the table in a way that ensures that all will have enough and no one will be left out.

We are asked as a body (that is, the members of the congregation who are gathered for worship) to make sure that there is plenty to go around and that we do not sate ourselves at the expense of others. Finally, Paul concludes, wait for one another when you come together. Let everyone share in the meal so that the vision of God's kingdom may be proclaimed among you!

Examining Ourselves: A Method for Taking Inventory

Paul's observations on the practices of the Corinthian community are also an invitation to us to examine our practices. Congregational leaders can facilitate table-centered renewal in a faith community by inviting members to take a careful inventory of their current practices. One way to begin this process is to review the passage from 1 Corinthians.

Examining Table Habits

Directions: Encourage participants to approach the text with an openness to new ways of seeing the dynamics, power structures, and relationships within the text. The following questions outline one way to read and interpret the claims of 1 Corinthians.

1. Read 1 Corinthians 11:17-22.

   • Describe what is going on in the church in Corinth.
   • What kind of table practices are pictured in the text?

2. Read 1 Corinthians 11:23-26.

   • What seems to be the purpose of this passage?
   • How do the Words of Institution function here? What is their role in the broader narrative?

3. Read 1 Corinthians 11:27-32.

   • What are examples of unworthy eating in the Corinthian community?
   • What is the purpose of judgment in this case?

After discussing the biblical assessment of communion practices, the group can turn its attention to its own setting. First, the group should ask who is gathering around the table. Does the assembly include a diversity of people from the surrounding community, or is the gathering primarily a collection of like-minded people? In Corinth, the community clearly included different socioeconomic groups as well as people with varied theological understandings (who were loyal to different leaders associated with the community). The problem in Corinth was not lack of diversity but the fact that the table was not serving its primary purpose of unifying people of differing backgrounds and interest groups.

Taking inventory in one's own congregation begins with honesty about who is gathering around the table and then proceeds to reflection on ways that table practices can welcome and include a wider variety of people from neighborhoods surrounding the church.

Second, reflection on our own table practices requires that we examine our own ethical practices and assumptions about eating and drinking. How do the actions at table in the church relate to the needs of people in the surrounding community to receive basic meals? The description of the Corinth community can help us assess our own practices. At the core of Paul's critique is a fundamental theological conviction that gathering around the table in remembrance of the Lord Jesus is integrally connected to acts of hospitality and sharing. Those who have plenty to eat and drink are instructed to share with those who have little.

What would such a gathering look like in the context of most congregations today? At the table and throughout life, there are to be no divisions among us. All are welcome. In some places, changing our habits may simply lead to opening the doors of the church and encouraging wider participation in the community by the regular members of the congregation and by others who live nearby. I recently visited a wealthy downtown church in a major city. At the early Sunday morning service that met in the chapel, I found myself sitting between older women in fur coats and homeless people bundled in old surplus coats who were glad to escape the cold of the street for at least a brief service. As the communion plates were passed down the aisle, we turned to our neighbors and invited them to share in the body of Christ. At the very least, sharing bread and wine with those whom we often ignore can lead us to consider our preconceptions about one another, biases that are often perpetuated by a society that rewards one's ability to produce in ways that the market validates. While it was clear that distinct separations existed in the sanctuary, the pastor and elders in the church modeled a spirit of equanimity and equality in welcoming all to the sanctuary and inviting all those present to the table. A church that works intentionally to bring people of different classes, races, and belief systems together will undoubtedly discover, like the Corinthians, that table practices and customs may divide us from one another. The words of Paul to Corinth surely remind us that the table should be a source for unity rather than for perpetuating false divisions.

In denominations that have reached agreement on sharing communion with other church bodies, living out these agreements can lead to cooperative ministry and deepen relationships among members of neighboring congregations. These experiences are crucial in broadening our horizons and helping us recognize the theological truth that the communion table does not belong to us. As we broaden our practices at the table and enlarge our vision of the place of the sacrament of communion in the life of the church, we discover how the table becomes an interpretive lens for our experiences outside the church and our service and engagement in the world.

Just as the table teaches us that there are to be no divisions among people, it reminds us that there is no distinction between the communion table and our dining tables. In a poor parish in Brazil, parishioners were invited to bring their coffee mugs to church with them the following week, when the congregation would celebrate the Lord's Supper. During the communion service they were invited to bring their mugs to the table, where juice was poured into the cups from the large communion pitcher. During coming months, members of the congregation told the pastor of new ways they thought about their own drinking habits when they were at home. When they drank coffee in their homes, they recalled the experience of coming to the table. In this process, their own coffee cups became a sign of the sacred and served as constant reminders of the presence of Christ not only at the table in church but at their own dining table.[1] These connections between the table in the sanctuary and the other tables around which we gather are central to seeing the world through our experiences around the communion table.

Another tangible response to the Corinthian survey and our own assessments of congregational life is to recover a clearer role for food in the communion meal itself. It is clear from the Corinthian text that this gathering around the table looked more like sharing a potluck dinner than eating a crouton of bread and sipping a thimbleful of juice or wine, as is the custom in many congregations these days. Food and drink are a part of the act of remembering and celebrating when we come to the table. It is not just in Corinth that Eucharist included a variety of foods. Justin Martyr's description of communion practices in the second century indicated that leftovers were to be taken to widows, prisoners, and the sick so that they would have something to eat. The table for Justin was a major source of food, which was distributed (and redistributed). Throughout the early church, a wide variety of eating and drinking practices were associated with gathering around the table to remember the Lord Jesus. In some places the communion meal was limited to bread and wine, but in other settings it likely included water, milk, honey, oil, olives, salt, and even a full meal.[2]

I am not suggesting a dramatic reformation of what we eat when we come to the communion table. Historical developments over the centuries reduced the meal to bread and wine.[3] However, I am underscoring the historic role of bread and cup that is central to the actions and practices at table. In many traditions, an emphasis on the spiritual dimensions of communion seems to overshadow the basic physical actions of breaking, pouring, passing, eating, and drinking. The reading from 1 Corinthians requires us to look closely at our eating practices, our ability to share our resources, and our willingness to welcome those who are different from us in a spirit of hope and trust that the table habits we practice will serve to unite us in the life of Christ.

We can discover in other ways the connection between eating at the table and sharing our bread with others in the community. In my former congregation, young children gathered in the narthex at the entrance to the sanctuary while the offering was being taken. As the congregation rose to sing a doxology, the children came down the aisles of the church. The first ones carried the communion elements—a plate with a loaf of bread, a pitcher filled with juice, an empty chalice. Other children carried bags of groceries and placed them around the communion table. The groceries were part of our ongoing collection to support the food bank in our neighborhood. While it was more work to bring the food into the sanctuary and carry it back out again, it added a tangible reminder to our prayers: "Give us who are fed at his hand, grace to share our bread with the hungry and with the hungry of heart."[4]

The beatitudes in the Gospel of Luke reflect Jesus's concern for the poor with the striking claim: "Blessed are you who are poor, for yours is the kingdom of God" (Luke 6:20). While Matthew may choose to qualify this notion as "poor in spirit," at the very least our prayers at the table can point to the physical needs of the hungry in our congregation, our community, and the world.

Connecting the table to other actions in the congregation may require only simple steps. We can connect the prayer and actions at the table to ministry done in the congregation's soup kitchen. In some congregations the bread on the communion table is the same as the bread offered in a soup kitchen. In settings where bread is baked for communion, additional loaves can be baked for feeding programs, and all the bread could be brought forward at the time of communion. At the very least, the prayers at the table can acknowledge and include those in the congregation and community who do not have enough to eat.

Congregations may want to explore ways the communion table can be connected with other tables. The communion plate (or paten) and pitcher (or flagon) may be used in a feeding program. Creating associations between the service at the communion table and service at other tables is a central way of connecting the practices of eating at table with the imperative to share our resources with others.

A collection plate could be placed near the communion table in congregations where worshipers come forward for communion, giving communicants the opportunity to donate to a particular feeding program. Such direct connections open people's imaginations, so that like Robert, whose story is told at the beginning of the chapter, they will begin to recognize opportunities during their work and in their daily lives.

At an emerging worship service in an Episcopal church in New York City, the congregation came forward to receive the communion elements. Once everyone was served, the table was quickly transformed. During the closing hymn, trays of pita bread, bowls of hummus, and glasses of lemonade were brought out and set on the table. At the end of the service, worshipers were invited back to the table for a time of fellowship around this simple meal. Friends and strangers stood together around the table to eat and converse.

To my great surprise, a former neighbor of mine in Tacoma, Washington, greeted me at the table. We had gone in separate directions but were reunited as we gathered around the table.

With Glad and Generous Hearts

While the congregation in Corinth serves as a classic example of malpractice, the witness and example of those in the first Christian communities serve as a primary illustration of best practice. The book of Acts portrays the rapid growth of the first Christian communities. In his description of Pentecost, Luke outlines the response of those who heard Peter's sermon. Three thousand people were suddenly added to the small collection of weary and frightened disciples who had gathered in the upper room. This burgeoning group devoted itself to specific tasks: "to the apostles' teaching and fellowship, to the breaking of bread and the prayers" (Acts 2:42).

We can identify the place of Word and Sacrament at the center of this movement. The Word centers on the apostles' testimony to the teaching and example of Jesus, while the breaking of the bread and the prayers point to the place of communion in the early Christian community. The vibrant life of this community does not stop there. Luke goes on to report that the sense of community was so strong that people pooled their assets and shared what they had with one another. Those in need found resources within the community. "Day by day, as they spent much time together in the temple, they broke bread at home and ate their food with glad and generous hearts, praising God and having the goodwill of all the people. And day by day the Lord added to their number those who were being saved" (Acts 2:46-47).

Here is a formula for church growth that is far different from and far more radical than what we discover in many church-growth handbooks. While we may not be ready and willing to embrace the communitarian enterprise, we can at least identify some of the ingredients that were transformative. The very act of gathering around the table is clearly central to the life of the community. While some interpreters may identify different nuances in the reference to breaking bread (which occurs twice, in verses 42 and 46, in this brief description), it remains integral to the event of Pentecost and in the subsequent description of life in the community. It signifies that gathering at the table cannot be understood as an add-on to our worship services, but that from the beginnings of Christianity, breaking bread together was a constitutive and basic pattern.

Another gleaning from the text in Acts is that a willingness to share our belongings can lead to wide-ranging transformation. Because basic needs were met for all, people were able to gather with glad and generous hearts in thanksgiving for the work the Spirit was prompting in the community. An invitation to the table can become an invitation to share in ways that allow people to experience fullness and joy. Recently I took a trip with my son to visit sites where he had been working in the Dominican Republic. We traveled up to a small town in the mountains, where we stayed with the family that had cared for him during his previous time in the Dominican Republic. When we arrived, we were welcomed with open arms and given heaping bowls of rice, beans, and eggplant. After a couple of days, we discovered that our host family was short on resources. Work had been scarce that month, and money, even for food, was limited. The opportunity to share our possessions came as a gift. My son, the daughter of the family, and I walked down the street to the marketplace to buy supplies. A spirit of abundance seized us, and we filled bags of food to take back to the house. The gift of hospitality in the household and the gift of sharing possessions "as any had need" led to meals filled with glad and generous hearts. I also observed that at nearly every meal, others in the neighborhood came and ate with us.

Searching for Christ

In spite of distinct theological differences that remain between denominations, Christians are united in believing that the risen Christ meets us as we gather around the communion table. Together we share a conviction that as bread is broken and wine is poured, we will encounter Christ in our midst. This core belief unites us as followers of Jesus Christ, despite differences in language and table practices. We will explore different customs in greater depth at a later point, but our aim now is to show how the experience of meeting Christ at table is connected to discovering the presence of Christ at other times and places in our lives. In this way, the communion table serves as a place of discovery that helps us sort through and identify our religious experiences.

In a well-known passage in Matthew 25, Jesus instructs his followers about where they will be able to find him. Jesus's words to his followers come at a time of conflict in Jerusalem. Matthew places this message in the last week of Jesus's ministry. In the face of trouble and as a death plot unfolds, Jesus offers a parable, a dreamlike scenario. Imagine that a judgment day is coming. All the nations have gathered and are waiting to meet with the king. Little do they know that everyone is about to receive unexpected news. On the one hand, the righteous are welcomed and received. This new kingdom, this world prepared before all time, is handed over to them in a nearly comic scene. This was apparently no goal-oriented, purpose-driven group. The righteous look at one another in bewilderment during the king's declaration and begin to mutter aloud, "Lord, when did we ever see you or feed you or give you something to drink or clothe you or visit you in prison or welcome you?" (v. 37, paraphrased).

You can almost hear them as they say to one another, "We are glad to come into this new world but cannot remember doing anything to deserve it." At this point, the king looks them straight in the eye and declares: "Truly, I tell you, just as you did it to one of the least of these who are members of my family, you did it to me" (v. 40).

At this point in the passage, the nervousness of the other group becomes apparent. I can imagine the ecclesiastical bureaucrats, committee junkies, purity-code police, and theological nitpickers immediately lodging a protest. "Lord, we never saw you. We were busy defending your church, enforcing our rules, keeping misfits outside the doors, promoting church growth, dealing with budget shortages, and attending to church business." Then the king turns and declares: "Go away. Go back to what you were doing. Go on about your business, for since you did not look for me in the midst of the least of these, since you ignored my family, you never even noticed my presence."

This dramatic portrait is often used by preachers to make an emotional appeal about the importance of taking care of those in need. In some instances, this appeal is delivered with large doses of guilt-inducing language and an implied threat that God is going to get us if we don't take pity on those who are less fortunate. What is missing in this appeal is a recognition of the basic premise of this text. Jesus's message is not a motivational speech to get his followers to show a little compassion once in a while. Instead, it is a radical claim that if we want to encounter Christ, we will need to leave our church buildings and embrace the poor, hungry, sick, imprisoned, and destitute. Our service to them is not simply about generous acts of compassion on our part. It is about learning to see and recognize Christ. This discovery begins at the table and extends into the world. According to the Gospel, it is the least of these who offer us a chance to discover Christ's presence. Rather than reinforcing the self-centered notion that our often limited generosity is a blessing for those less fortunate than ourselves, these people become a source of revelation to us and point us to ways to connect our experiences around the table with our work and ministry in the world.

Extending the Table

From the outset, this book expands our notions of what it means to gather around the communion table in the sanctuary of the church. The shape of prayer at the table and the patterns of our gathering need critical analysis so that we can avoid the insular ways in which we sometimes gather. Rather than constituting a private activity for individuals, communion by its very nature brings people together to share bread that is broken and wine that is poured out. In this process, communion not only becomes an event in the life of the church; it becomes a paradigm for living in the world.

By paying close attention to the biblical models of gathering at table, we gain insight into ways to assess the strengths and weaknesses of the practices in our congregations. In this analysis, many of our assumptions may be dramatically challenged. Effective leaders go about this process slowly and continually, allowing the dramatic signs, symbols, actions, and events of those who gather around the table to take root in their lives. Extending metaphors, making connections, offering hospitality, and preaching sermons that reflect on these experiences enable congregations to embody central practices of Christian faith beyond the walls of the church.

Hymn for Reflection

Here in this place the new light is streaming,
now is the darkness vanished away;
see in this space our fears and our dreamings
brought here to you in the light of this day.
Gather us in, the lost and forsaken,
gather us in, the blind and the lame;
call to us now, and we shall awaken,
we shall arise at the sound of our name.

We are the young, our lives are a mystery,
we are the old who yearn for your face;
we have been sung throughout all of history,
called to be light to the whole human race.
Gather us in, the rich and the haughty,
gather us in, the proud and the strong;
give us a heart, so meek and so lowly,
give us the courage to enter the song.

Here we will take the wine and the water,
here we will take the bread of new birth,
here you shall call your sons and your daughters,
call us anew to be salt for the earth.
Give us to drink the wine of compassion,
give us to eat the bread that is you;
nourish us well, and teach us to fashion
lives that are holy and hearts that are true.

Not in the dark of buildings confining,
Not in some heaven, light years away—
here in this place the new light is shining,
now is the kingdom, and now is the day.
Gather us in and hold us forever
gather us in and make us your own;
gather us in, all peoples together,
fire of love in our flesh and our bone.[5]

Questions for Discussion

1. What is your "meal pattern"? When do you celebrate the sacrament, and how often? Who is able to receive the elements (keep in mind age, membership, or other criteria)? What do you use for bread and fruit of the vine? What is the meaning behind the use of wine? Is grape juice different, and if so, in what way?

2. How does the Lord's Supper "happen" in your church? Who prepares the elements and table, and who cleans up afterward? What do you do with the elements that have not been consumed, and what might you do with them? Who serves them to the congregation, and in what fashion? How are the elements served and received: do people receive the elements in the pews, walk up to receive them, stand, kneel at an altar rail, or sit at tables—or receive in some other way? Does the pastor receive the bread and cup first or last—and what does that order say?

3. Consider the "radical claim that if we want to encounter Christ, we will need to leave our church buildings and embrace the poor, hungry, sick, imprisoned, and destitute" (page 31). What does this mean? Do you agree or disagree? Read texts such as Isaiah 35:1-6 and Luke 4:14-21, and especially Matthew 25:31-46 to think about this claim.

4. Recite or sing together the Hymn for Reflection on pages 32–33. How do these words reflect on the chapter you have just read or the conversation you have shared? Do they leave you energized or troubled? Who are you among the gathered? Whom does Christ's call to gather include in the life of your congregation?

CHAPTER 3

Re-membering the Body of Christ

Everliving God, author of creation, we give you thanks for your gift of water that brings life and refreshes the earth. We bless and praise you, for by water and the Word we are cleansed from sin and receive everlasting life.[1]

A Place to Begin

"Remember your baptism and be thankful in the name of the Father, and of the Son, and of the Holy Spirit." The words echoed in the sanctuary over and over again as people slowly moved down the aisles of the church. Near the chancel, each person stopped at the font, dipped a hand in the water, touched hand to forehead, and received a blessing from one of the pastors leading the service. For a moment, I wondered what people were actually remembering. It was an ecumenical gathering. Some present were baptized as infants, some as children and teens, others as adults. What is it that people were being asked to remember? While some might actually have been reflecting on their own baptisms, others were renewing their baptismal vows by gathering around the font in a collective expression of their faith.

I decided to interview people about their baptismal memories in the small congregation where I worship. In this predominantly African American church, members come from a wide variety of denominational backgrounds. When I asked them to reflect on memorable baptismal experiences, I heard different narratives. Lela spoke of her own baptism:

> I am the daughter of a Baptist preacher. I was ten years old in 1933. I was baptized in a creek in late October. I can see my father with hip boots on and a crooked staff, and the deacons walk out into the water. I had been to the mourner's bench for confession, so I was ready to be baptized. After the cold water, they receive you and wrap you in blankets to take you to the church. It was a solemn and profound experience.

This vivid memory carries tangible, sensual elements: the cold creek and the warm blanket, a father to baptize you and a new family to embrace you.

But for Lela, the memory is not simply of a static, long-ago event. The creek remains a place of pilgrimage. "I go back now and just stand at the creek and look." Returning to the location of her baptism provides a sense of identity that keeps the experience fresh and vibrant. For her, remembering includes other active responses. She tells me, "I bought a picture that reminded me of my baptism in a creek." The picture acts as an icon as it prompts her to keep her baptismal experience present. It serves as a reservoir from which to draw strength. It is a visual expression of Martin Luther's declaration that there is no greater source of comfort in life than the words "I am baptized."

Eleanor shares a different memory of baptism:

> I have two children who were baptized here. My daughter was baptized here. They used to sprinkle right there in front at church. I dressed them up in white. There were eleven years between our children. My son was baptized earlier than the girl. He was still a baby—less than a year. Baptism always has been a joyous occasion.

The act of remembering baptism brings back the experiences of her children's acceptance into the life of the faith community. Baptism is an occasion of celebration and joy. Her reflections become all the more poignant as she immediately follows her observations about the joyfulness of the baptismal occasions with a reflection on life's transitions: "Now my daughter is deceased. She was buried in this church. She became a minister, but then died in 2002. I brought her back here to be buried where she was baptized."

Here, remembering baptism is part of a lifelong journey that embraces joyful celebrations of new life and baptismal gifts expressed and lived out in ordained ministry, and encompasses even death. Together, these boundaries of life and death are brought to the baptismal font, the place of memory and experience that holds them all together. Her reflections echo the language of the liturgy in the service of witness to the resurrection:

> O God,
> before whom generations rise and pass away,
> we praise you for all your servants
> who, having lived this life in faith,
> now live eternally with you.
> Especially we thank you for your servant
> Whose baptism is now complete in death.[2]

The language of this prayer surrounds our lives and encompasses our memories so that, even in times of loss, we are immersed in waters that bring healing and renew hope. Here the act of remembering encompasses a life journey of faith. Remembering is grounded in the event of baptism, yet extends through a lifetime.

At the font, remembering our baptism is less a cognitive experience of trying to dredge up the recollections of one specific event than a way of picturing all those who gather at the font in hope and thanksgiving for God's blessing. Thus, every baptism is an opportunity for all who gather to participate actively by renewing our baptismal vows and affirming our faith as followers of Jesus Christ. Together, we share in this proclamation and witness that God claims us as sons and daughters and joins us together. There, surrounded by the cloud of witnesses, we gather as the church, the re-membered body of Christ.

Re-membering Our Path from Font to Table

Baptism and communion as sacraments of the church are events around which the community gathers. Through water, word, bread, and wine, people of faith experience the presence of the risen Christ. At table and font, the Christian story is proclaimed as it is associated with this water, this bread, and this wine. Each time we gather around font and table, we are asked to remember.

Memory and hope are central themes in our prayers. This sense of hope often carries with it an anticipation of a day and time when all God's children will gather in thanksgiving and praise to break bread and share the cup. Our hope holds up a vision of a banquet meal where all the saints will eat and drink in thanksgiving and praise for God's goodness to us. Hope points toward a future when our divisions will end and God will embrace us as the one body of Christ. Hope is a shared vision of God's future.

Even though hope may be less than tangible, memory seems even more elusive. What is it that we are remembering at the table? The words of Jesus reported by the apostle Paul in 1 Corinthians 11 provide a kind of framework: "Do this in remembrance of me."[3] In the Gospel of Luke, these words occur in the middle of the Passover meal Jesus shares with his disciples in the upper room on the night before his crucifixion in Jerusalem. Since time travel does not allow us to go back to this event, it is clear that we are not trying to remember our participation in that particular meal. Instead, in the midst of the gathering of this family, we remember not to go back to a distant past but to discover our identity as brothers and sisters of Jesus Christ. To do this in remembrance of Christ is to claim our place at the table in light of our baptism.

For Christians, communion is also not a memory of a Passover meal we have shared together. While some congregations have experimented with piecing together parts of a Passover meal as part of their gatherings on Maundy Thursday, this event is completely different from the gathering of Jesus and the disciples in Jerusalem. No attempt to recreate this setting will allow us access to the meal that this group of devout Jews shared together as a part of their pilgrimage to Jerusalem and their prayers for the renewal of their faith community. Furthermore, it is unlikely that the rituals that we recreate will share much similarity to the Passover meal in the upper room.

Another proposal for solving the riddle of the meaning of "Do this in remembrance of me" is to shift the focus from the Passover meal to the crucifixion. This shift of location has become so commonplace in some congregations that it is almost taken for grated that the act of remembering is associated with the events of Good Friday. In this scenario, the preacher and presider provide verbal cues that encourage the participants to associate the bread and cup with the suffering of Jesus on the cross at Calvary. The link in this chain is usually a particular theological interpretation of the Corinthians text. The bread is associated with Jesus's body that is given for us, and the cup is associated with a new covenant in Christ's blood. The primary purpose of gathering at the communion table then is for individual members of the congregation to think about Jesus's sacrifice while they eat and drink.

Both the Passover and Good Friday proposals run contrary to the understanding of remembrance that lies at the center of remembering one's baptism. Is there a way to build on this sense of an active, communal understanding of remembrance? The 1 Corinthians text itself provides helpful clues to guide us. First, in the previous chapter we discovered that the words of institution are embedded in a discussion of the ethical actions of providing and sharing food. To share communion is to provide food for all those who gather at the table. Those who bring much are instructed to share their food with those who have little. For Paul, this is the very basis of communion. In his instructions to the church in Corinth, he makes it clear that this is the nonnegotiable element of the Lord's Supper (or to put it another way, without an equal distribution of food, the meal is not communion). From this passage, we can see that Paul places equal food for all at the center of communion. Rather than particular words or specific thoughts, it is the actions of sharing and eating that illumine the experience of communion. These common acts lead theologian Laurence Stookey to declare: "The words 'do this' are even more crucial than 'in remembrance of me.' (Many Protestants thus have the wrong words carved into their communion tables.)"[4]

For Paul, the Words of Institution are surrounded by a discourse on ethics. First comes a critical observation of the Corinthian community's malpractice. Afterward comes the command to discern the body. This discernment is no private, individual act of introspection but an examination of the community's treatment of those who are hungry.

The Pauline language of remembrance prompts an active form of remembering. In this sense, to *re-member* is to bring back or reassemble. When you do this (share your food), then you are about the business of re-membering the presence of Christ. Or, as theologian Don Saliers instructs those gathering at the table: Do this for the re-membering of me.[5] Equally significant, this language underscores the church's act of reconstituting or reconfiguring itself as the body of Christ as it gathers at the table to eat bread and drink wine.

The Greek word for "remembering" in this text is *anamnesis* and involves actively making the past present. In English, we know the cognate forms of the word mostly through its antonym, "amnesia"—forgetfulness. Those who experience amnesia can no longer bring back and live out of shared experiences. This form of forgetfulness carries with it a sense of lack of participation in one's surroundings due to the absence of shared memories that bring and hold people together. Those who have experienced temporary forms of amnesia attest that the return of memory comes as both gift and miracle in restoring them to their place in the community.

From Amnesia to *Anamnesis*

I sat near the back of the sanctuary where a small group of people gathered for worship. The guest minister announced that it was communion Sunday. After the sermon, he left the chancel and stood behind the communion table. Awkwardly, he stared at the printed order of worship and proceeded to stumble through a reading of the communion prayer. There were no gestures, no actions, just a long text that had to be completed before getting on with the service. In my travels around the church, this practice is far from an anomaly. Where a full eucharistic prayer is offered, the prayer is often a matter of endurance. We seem to have forgotten how to break bread! How did this collective form of amnesia overcome us? I believe that among the reasons are modern spiritualities that begin with individualistic, privatized notion of faith. When we start with ourselves and our own needs, it becomes more difficult for the community to eat and drink communally as a way of re-membering or bringing together again the body of Christ.

In contrast, *anamnesis* seeks to embody a way of enacting the presence of Christ among us. A eucharistic prayer becomes an occasion for prodding and provoking the memory of those who gather, in order that we may come to the table as the body of Christ. In this approach, the role of recollection is to (re)discover our identity and place in the story of God's redemptive work in the world.

Amnesia is not a new problem, however. Scripture speaks of the pervasive forgetfulness that can cause us to miss out on the basic connection between a new understanding and a new way of acting. In the days after the experiences of Holy Week, the disciples huddled in fear. They had heard *reports* of an empty tomb and sightings of Christ. Mary Magdalene had announced that she had seen the risen Lord when she went to visit the tomb on the first day of the week. According to the Gospel of John, when Peter and the other disciple (the one whom Jesus loved) had heard the news, they had run to the tomb and found it empty. But Mary had stayed in the garden, and through her tears she had encountered the risen Christ who had sent her to tell the disciples of his resurrection.

The news of this sighting did not erase the disciples' fear and confusion. Uncertainty and angst remained. They gathered behind locked doors and wondered what to do next. John describes the disciples' transition from anxiety to hope. Suddenly, Jesus came and stood among them. Jesus's first words are: "Peace be with you." This greeting of peace is followed by the gift of life as Jesus breathes on the disciples, blesses them, and bestows on them the gift of the Holy Spirit. The disciples were filled with joy.

In spite of this seminal experience, not all of Jesus's followers are convinced of the resurrection. Thomas, who had been absent from the earlier gathering, remained uncertain. He wanted firsthand experience and an encounter with the risen Christ. John tells us of a gathering a week later when the disciples, including Thomas, met again in the house. John uses the exchange between Jesus and Thomas as a witness to the resurrection, not only for Thomas but especially for those "who have not seen and yet have come to believe" (John 20:29).

The story could end at that point. And yet, astonishingly, John adds an afterword that speaks directly to the themes of forgetting, remembering, and embodying our beliefs in acts of compassion. Peter leads a group of the disciples on a fishing expedition. Whether this outing represents a return to the past cannot be determined from the text, but the nighttime expedition on the water is highly unsuccessful. Then a stranger appears on the shore and inquires about their catch of fish. "Try casting the net on the other side of the boat," he instructs them. Miraculously, they find that suddenly their nets are full of fish. In fact, John reports the number of large fish as 153. Some Greek zoologists at the time estimated that there were 153 species of fish, so the number of fish in the nets represents the total range of species.[6]

It is Peter who recognizes that this bounteous catch comes from the presence of the risen Christ. He grabs some clothes, jumps into the water, and swims ashore. As the disciples all gather on the beach, they discover that supper is waiting for them. A charcoal fire is burning (with fish already grilling!), and bread is heating up over the fire. Jesus invites the disciples to come and eat. Then, "Jesus came and took the bread and gave it to them, and did the same with the fish" (John 21:13). The language directly (and intentionally) pushes us to remember a previous experience. In this case, John 6 serves as a backdrop. There, at the feeding of the five thousand, the same meal is presented. The fish and loaves offered from a boy's lunch provided lunch for the memorable feast. In this case, the language takes on eucharistic tones: "Then Jesus took the loaves, and when he had given thanks, he distributed them to those who were seated; so also the fish, as much as they wanted" (John 6:11). It is worth noting that Jesus's actions in the synoptic accounts of the feeding of the five thousand are reflected in the basic pattern of the eucharistic prayer. Jesus takes the bread, blesses it, breaks it, and gives it to the disciples. Liturgical scholars recognize that these four actions provide a shape for the liturgy.[7]

Here on the shore in Galilee, a breakfast meal with the risen Christ is an occasion for remembering other experiences and shared meals. One gathering alludes to earlier ones. In the simple telling of this story, the author of the Gospel links several meals together as signs of the presence of Christ along the way of the disciples' journeys.

The Gospels not only link meals with the risen Christ together. They also link these meals with ways to respond to Christ's presence. The meal in John 21 is linked to a set of ethical imperatives. After breakfast, Peter is instructed to feed others. In a repetitive exchange, Jesus links the notion of loving him with the imperative to share food with others: "Feed my sheep" (v. 17). Here the action of the shared meal (that in itself is a way of remembering) leads to a vision and command to tend to the needs of others in our communities.

Re-membering as Embodiment

By now, it should be clear that this way of remembering is far different from the usual methods of trying to think our way back to some earlier time. Re-membering is a way of sharing experiences that are linked to past events and yet point to future gatherings. In the life of a congregation, finding direct ways to make these links is crucial to uncovering the basic patterns of eucharistic prayer. Here is one brief story of a way to bring these patterns to the surface in a congregation's life and worship.

On the first Sunday of November, our congregation gathered to celebrate the feast of All Saints. This in itself was an unusual occurrence in a Presbyterian church. However, in a congregation where longtime members were dying at a rapid pace (thirty-five during my first year as pastor), the notion of taking time to remember those who had gone before us became a favorite celebration. In planning the service, we looked for ways to find a balance between past and present, between remembering and acting.

During the service, our eucharistic prayer included a time of thanksgiving and remembering for those who had died during the past year. Often, the sermon for the day mentioned the importance of carrying forward the legacy of those who had gone before us as witnesses. Immediately after the service, we gathered downstairs in fellowship hall for a congregational meal. It was the usual church potluck with the odd assortment of Jell-O salads, green-bean casseroles, and a vast assortment of desserts. We took the leftover communion bread and added it to the buffet tables as a way of extending the Lord's table to the other tables where we gathered to eat.

Then came the awards ceremony. Each year, we honored a small number of living saints among us. These were long-term members whose lives of service and dedication made them mentors for the rest of us. They had offered years of volunteer service in the free medical clinic, decades of singing in the choir, and ongoing participation in Habitat for Humanity. In each case, we found a simple way to say thank you. We presented each saint with a simple candle with a cross and expressed our gratitude with these words: "We give thanks for the light of Christ that we have seen in your life."

I remain astounded at the power of a gesture this simple. Those who had given decades of service to the church were deeply moved and grateful, while those of us who were newcomers to the congregation gained a deeper sense of the congregational identity. We learned from one another ways to connect remembering and action as we embody faith in service to the community. Re-membering is a way of sharing experiences that are linked to past events and yet point to future enactments. When we celebrated All Saints' Sunday together, we discovered ways to re-member that connected us as a community of memory and hope.

Please Pass the Vignettes!

One more Gospel narrative portrays the links between remembering, breaking bread, and acting ethically. The Gospel of Luke tells of the encounter between Jesus and Zacchaeus, chief tax collector in the important trade city of Jericho. Luke tells us that he was rich. When he hears that Jesus is coming to town, Zacchaeus longs to see this famous teacher. Even though Zacchaeus is a rich and powerful figure in the community, no one in the crowd is making room for him to catch a glimpse of Jesus.

Zacchaeus takes matters into his own hands. He forgets about his prestige and standing in the community. His desire to see Jesus is so great that he runs ahead of the crowd and climbs a sycamore tree so that he will not miss out on this opportunity to see Jesus pass through the city. When Jesus comes to the tree where Zacchaeus is resting, he stops and announces, "Zacchaeus, hurry and come down; for I must stay at your house today" (Luke 19:5).

The people of Jericho are shocked. After all, Zachaeus is clearly a sinner. He has been in cahoots with the Romans. It is bad enough for Jesus to acknowledge him, but to go to his house and to break bread with him? They begin to grumble and accuse Jesus of associating with the wrong people.

At this point, Zacchaeus steps forward and announces on his own that he is going to change his ways. "Look, half of my possessions, Lord, I will give to the poor; and if I have defrauded anyone of anything, I will pay back four times as much" (v. 8). In Luke, Zacchaeus's declaration that he will change his life is placed directly in contrast with the story of the rich young ruler in the preceding chapter. Like Zacchaeus, the rich young ruler is a successful man. Similarly, he seeks out Jesus to learn how to inherit eternal life. In contrast to Zacchaeus, the rich young ruler is devoutly religious. He knows and follows the commandments. He declares that he has kept them his entire life but that something is still lacking. Jesus instructs him, "Sell all that you own and distribute the money to the poor" (Luke 18:22). Luke tells us that this good religious man, who longed for the secret to eternal life, went away sad because he was very rich. It is one thing to follow the rules of the commandments and something else completely to change your life.

As far as we know, Zacchaeus lacks religious devotion. He is considered an outcast, a sinner in the community. Suddenly, though, faced with Christ's invitation to share a meal, he becomes connected with God and with the deep needs of the poor. All the things that he owned and had worked for so hard during his life did not seem nearly so important to him. The opportunity to break bread with Jesus opened up a desire to reach out to those who were poor and those whom he had defrauded. Jesus announces to Zacchaeus and all who surround him, "Today salvation has come to this house, because he too is a son of Abraham" (Luke 19:9).

These contrasting portraits point the way to eternal life. Jesus welcomes Zacchaeus to embrace the chance to reorient his life by giving to the poor and sharing his wealth with those in need. The anticipated meal at table breaks open new ways of living and acting.

Re-membering the Future

In the old Scottish communion prayers, the Words of Institution were often repeated. They came at the beginning of the communion prayer and were sometimes spoken again in the middle and even at the close of the prayer. At the beginning of the prayer at table, the words "Do this in remembrance of me" frame the actions of the assembly, so that our remembering may shape us and we may be transformed in this process. In reflecting on this liturgy, John Knox (the leading reformer of the Church of Scotland) offers this observation:

> And as for the words of the Lord's Supper, we rehearse them, not because they should change the substance of the bread or wine, or that the repetition thereof, with the intent of the sacrifice, should make Sacrament . . . but they are read and pronounced, to teach us how to behave ourselves in that action, and Christ might witness unto our faith, as it were with his own mouth, that he hath ordained these signs to our spiritual use and comfort.[8]

Here, remembering takes on the character of training us how to act. This remembering builds on the Gospel narratives of the transformation of those who broke bread with Jesus. The apostle Paul offers words of exhortation to the church at Corinth to share food equitably with all who gather at table. This is the true Eucharist that embodies the remembrance of Jesus's breaking bread and sharing the cup with the disciples. For Peter, the bread and fish shared with the risen Christ evoke memories of the feeding of five thousand. At the same time, Peter hears Jesus's directive to feed others. For Zacchaeus, the possibility of dining with Jesus leads to new ways of sharing his wealth with those in his community.

These varieties of religious experience coalesce around a way of remembering that is embodied and transformative. Here, remembering is linked to the past, open to the present, and embracing of the future. Remembering your baptism with thanksgiving is a way of living the baptismal life in a community of faith. Likewise, *doing this* in remembrance of Christ provides direction in the lives of those who gather around the table. These sacraments of baptism and communion link us with the past, give us an identity, and point the way into a new future so that our communities of faith may become the body of Christ in the world.

Hymn for Reflection

At the font we start our journey,
in the Easter faith baptized;
doubts and fears no longer blind us,
by the light of Christ surprised.
Alleluia, alleluia!
Hope held out and realized.

At the pulpit we are fashioned
by the Easter tale retold
into witnesses and prophets,
by the power of Christ made bold.
Alleluia, alleluia!
Faith proclaimed, yet still untold.

At the altar we are nourished
with the Easter gift of bread;
in our breaking it to pieces
see the love of Christ outspread.

Alleluia, alleluia!
Life embraced, yet freely shed.

At the door we are commissioned,
now the Easter victory's won,
to restore a world divided
to the peace of Christ as one.
Alleluia, alleluia!
Easter's work must still be done.[9]

Questions for Discussion

1. Share memorable baptismal experiences. Why were they so memorable?

2. Jesus says, "Do this in remembrance of me." The word *remember* can be thought of as *re-member*, that is, putting the members back together. In the celebration of the Lord's Supper, what are we putting back together? Is it people (known and/or unknown to us), places, situations—or all of the above?

3. Read Joshua 3:7–4:7 in light of the All Saints observance and the gifting of living saints with light. What does this story say about remembering for us today? And what does it say about "re-membering the future"? How would the gift of remembering those who have contributed to your congregation's life and ministry be received in your community?

4. Recite or sing together the Hymn for Reflection on pages 47–48. How do these words reflect on the chapter you have just read or the conversation you have shared? The words of this hymn walk us through a sanctuary. Are these descriptions of place reminiscent of your worship space? Why or why not? Font, pulpit, and table are common and well-understood elements of our worship. Is the door a surprise? What does it suggest?

CHAPTER 4

Welcoming Friend and Stranger

Friends, this is the joyful feast of the people of God.
They will come from east and west,
And from north and south,
And sit at table in the kingdom of God.
> Invitation to the Lord's Table from the
> *Book of Common Worship*

The silver chalice on the communion table was engraved with the words "Dedicated by Jane. For all my friends." Every time we used it in a service, I wondered whether I should really be drinking from this chalice, since I had never met Jane. What idea of friendship and hospitality was reflected in the practice of sharing this cup? Who is really welcome at the communion table? Christian traditions have answered this question in different ways. At times, churches have enforced strict rules about participating in communion. Some traditions practiced a fencing of the table—extending the invitation only to those who had gone through examination and gained approval by clergy or sessions. (At times the Scottish church handed out communion tokens to grant access to the table.) Other traditions found other ways to limit participation at the table to members of their congregation.

In recent years, conversations are growing about who is welcome at the communion table. In these conversations, an "open table" is understood in widely differing ways. In some settings, an open table refers to the growing practice of ecumenical cooperation between members of congregations and different denominations who now are invited to gather at the table. (The Reformed-Lutheran agreement is a dramatic example of this cooperation.) In other settings the discussion of an open table seeks to challenge the historic practice of requiring baptism before communion. While we cannot address all the questions that surround the issue of the open table, this chapter explores the biblical foundations and issues of offering hospitality in table practices.

Scenes from the Gospel of Mark

All the Gospels frequently depict Jesus's meal practices as controversial. From early in his ministry, Jesus is accused of eating with the wrong people. Matthew's call is connected with this controversy. After a series of healings, a crowd in Capernaum gathers around Jesus to hear him teach. As Jesus walks along the seashore, he encounters Matthew at work in his tax booth. Matthew leaves behind his work and answers Jesus's call to follow him. Immediately, Jesus joins Matthew for dinner. Many other tax collectors and sinners gather around the table with Jesus and his disciples. The response of some religious leaders is decidedly negative. "Why does he eat with tax collectors and sinners?" (Mark 2:16). At stake are more than eating habits. The controversy is driven by concern about keeping Jewish purity codes. Contact with the impure (tax collectors and sinners) creates impurity. The result is that all who break bread together with those who are deemed unclean share in the violation of the purity codes. Thus, Jesus breaks strict religious rules to share a meal with Matthew and his friends. Jesus's response to the religious authorities who question this practice is that his ministry is precisely for those who are in need ("I have come to call not the righteous but sinners").

In Mark's Gospel the invitation to table fellowship involves two responses. First is a willingness to follow Jesus. Matthew's response to Jesus's call to discipleship leads directly to the table. Second, coming to the table involves joining a wide range of others who are hungry to hear the good news that Jesus announces to all. Accepting Jesus's invitation involves a personal decision and a willingness to be a part of a new community that gathers around the table.

These themes are underlined and broadened in another table controversy in the next chapter of Mark. Following the calling and commissioning of all the apostles, Jesus gathers with them in his home. Crowds surround them, making it difficult to eat. This time, Jesus is criticized for not eating with his biological family. "Your mother and your brothers and sisters are outside, asking for you" (Mark 3:32). This time, Jesus points to the solidarity of those who are at table with him. "The ones who gather here are my mother and my brothers, for whoever does God's will is a member of my family," he insists.

Here, table practices are pictured as defining a new sense of family. No longer are blood ties the only determinative factor. Kinship is replaced by shared commitments. Those who join in pursuit of God's will are family members.

These two meal stories at the beginning of Mark's Gospel serve to underscore the centrality of the practices of hospitality in Jesus's ministry. Jesus's table practices are not defined by religious law or family expectations. Instead, Jesus redefines table hospitality in terms of a willingness to respond to the gospel and to follow God's will. In light of our response to the gospel, whom will we invite to gather with us at the communion table?

Inviting Friends

In the Reformed tradition, actions in worship usually begin with a verse from Scripture. A call to worship from a biblical text is often the first sentence spoken in many services. Similarly, when it is time to gather around the table, Scripture provides a basis. Thus, the invitation to the table adapted from Luke 13 that begins this chapter deserves further reflection.

The invitation begins, "Friends, this is the joyful feast of the people of God." First, who are these friends? In light of our reading of Mark's Gospel, the invitation to "friends" takes on new meaning. In this context, friends are those who respond to Jesus's invitation to discipleship and who share a commitment to following

God's will. This notion of friendship critiques common assumptions about friendship. Friends are not defined as those whom we like, those with whom we agree, or even those with whom we share common interests. In fact, the meal scenes in the Gospel picture a scattered array of outsiders and questionable people who come together at table expressly to have conversation with Jesus. Here, friendship with Jesus Christ is determined by a willingness to listen and to follow God's will.

Friends—those with whom we agree and those with whom we disagree—are called together around the table to break bread and to share the cup as a common sign that our commitment to Christ surpasses all our differences of opinion on other topics. Lest this practice sound completely idealistic, note that this understanding of friendship presumes a willingness to get along even when we disagree. A quick look at the conflict in the early church points to ways that difficulties and disagreements were handled. In Acts 15, we read of two visions for the future of the church. Will circumcision be required for Gentile Christians? While this fiercely contested debate provides an endorsement for Paul's work with the Gentile community, it does not end the discussion. Instead, the early Christian community agrees to endorse the work of Paul and Barnabas while providing limited guidelines (avoid nonkosher food and fornication). The Christian family, established in baptism, is not about always agreeing or holding the same opinions. Instead, in the midst of disagreements, we are welcome at the table to share this meal with other friends of Jesus.

In our congregation during the season of Lent, we gathered each Thursday evening for a brief communion service. The service was enacted largely around the table, with a brief Scripture reading and message followed by an invitation to the table and the great prayer of thanksgiving. At the end of the prayer, we formed a large circle around the table. One by one, we served the bread to one another and passed the chalice around the circle. At one service, I noticed a couple who were undergoing a significant crisis in their marriage seated apart in the sanctuary. When we gathered around the table, the couple somehow ended up standing next to each other in the circle. In tears, they served each other. Around the table, their common commitment superseded their differences.

It is important to add that coming to the table and serving one another did not solve their marriage problems. Yet it underscored that in the midst of broken relationships, we can hold common commitments to Christ.

Around the table the gospel challenges our notions of kinship and friendship. In place of communities that are grounded in familial ties and shared interests and lifestyles, Jesus points to a table where people are united by their willingness to pursue God's reign in our world. As one communion hymn puts it: "As Christ breaks bread and bids us share, each proud division ends. The Love that made us, makes us one, and strangers now are friends."[1]

A Joyful Feast of the People of God?

Sometimes I wonder if talk of communion as a joyful feast is just church hyperbole run amok. In many congregations, the dark penitential mood of the communion service overwhelms any feelings of joy. Likewise, small crumbs of bread and tiny sips of juice or wine seem far removed from practices of feasting. What joyful feast can the church celebrate as it gathers around the table? By returning to Mark's Gospel, we can gain insight into sustaining joy in our table practices from the way Mark continues to place the practice of eating together at the center of the story of Jesus.

Following a series of reports of Jesus's healing, exorcism, and teaching, Mark offers two dramatic feast accounts. A feeding of four thousand follows the feeding of the five thousand. These two dramatic miracle stories present an invitation to share in surprisingly joyful feasts that bring together different groups of people. In the first account, Jesus returns from a brief respite and is immediately confronted by crowds from the surrounding villages. He begins to speak to the crowds and to teach them. As the hour becomes late, the disciples grow worried about how to feed the multitude. "Send them away," they tell Jesus so that the people can go into town and find something to eat. Jesus instructs the disciples to provide food for the crowd. The disciples do not have nearly enough cash on hand to buy food for this many people. Jesus sends them into the crowd to look for supplies, and the disciples come back with five loaves of bread and two fish. Hardly enough for a feast! The description is strikingly (and deliberately) similar to the basic actions at the communion table: Jesus takes the bread, blesses it, breaks it, and gives it to the disciples to share with the people. "And all ate and were filled" (Mark 6:42).

Scholars agree that the details of this first feeding story are provided to press the point that Jesus teaches and feeds a Jewish gathering. First, the account recalls earlier feeding stories in the Old Testament. In Exodus, God provides manna to sustain the Hebrew people in their wilderness wanderings. In 2 Kings, Elisha receives loaves of barley and fresh ears of grain and tells his servant to serve them to the one hundred men who are gathered, and the food is more than enough to feed them all. Jesus's feeding of the five thousand builds on these memorable stories. Here the Jewish crowd, the people of God, not only receive Jesus's word but also participate in a joyful, bountiful feast that ends with twelve baskets of leftovers to share with others. The twelve baskets provide food for each of the twelve tribes of Israel,[2] enough food for all God's people to eat together.

In Mark, after the feeding of the five thousand, Jesus crosses over the Sea of Galilee and arrives in Gennesaret. He is immediately confronted by crowds in search of healing. He is also confronted by Pharisees from Jerusalem, who again accuse him of unclean eating practices. Jesus responds by claiming that these religious leaders have abandoned God's commandments by preoccupation with purity codes. Jesus declares that it is not people and external things that create impurity. Rather, defilement comes from our own evil intentions.

As Jesus enters the region of Tyre, a Syrophoenician woman who begs Jesus to heal her daughter quickly tests Jesus's message. She argues with Jesus to share at least the crumbs of bread with Gentiles. Shortly after this exchange, Jesus's mission to the Gentiles culminates with a second feast, the feeding of four thousand. In this account, the crowd again gathers around Jesus. Jesus expresses his concern for the crowd's hunger, for they have been here three days without anything to eat. Once again, the disciples have no idea what to do. Again, loaves of bread are found. This time the number is seven. Again, Jesus takes the bread, gives thanks (blesses), breaks, and gives. Similarly, a few fish are shared. This time, the leftovers make up seven baskets of food. For biblical writers, seven represents a perfect number, completion, so the message is clearly that there is food enough for all people—since Jews and Gentiles are both the people of God.[3]

These two feasts in Mark's Gospel are signs that the invitation to God's reign extends to all people. The invitation to the meal is an invitation to a new community. During the meal Jesus takes, blesses, breaks, and gives so that all will be able to eat. These meals form a new community of God's people. Old practices of separation and isolation are left behind to make room for new ways of sharing life together.

Finally, the meals are not an end in themselves but create a sense of anticipation. The joyful feasts are marked by the surprise of those who receive food to eat, by the inclusion of crowds and Gentiles, and by a hopeful expectation of meals to come. When we declare that this is the joyful feast of the people of God, we share in this drama. We respond in surprise at this invitation to gather with strangers around the table. And we come with hearts full of expectation for receiving and sharing.

From East and West and North and South

At a recent service in our seminary chapel, we heard stories from faculty members and students who had spent time in Korea. Their presentations underscored the ongoing tension between North and South Korea that continues to divide families. Syngman Rhee, who was a distinguished professor of evangelism and mission and whose life story and tireless advocacy for reconciliation in Korea have shaped his work and ministry, led our communion prayer. In the words of invitation to the table, his repeated assertion that people will gather from south and north to eat together carried new and explosive implications.

Thus, the invitation to gather at the table holds the possibility of reorienting our way of looking at the world. Like the Gospel meals themselves, the invitation to the table includes all people. On the surface, Jesus in the Gospel of Luke symbolizes this invitation by welcoming people from all ends of the earth to eat in God's kingdom.

On closer inspection, this citation from Luke 13:29 quickly becomes problematic. The text is embedded in a passage of judgment. The thanksgiving for God's goodness from Psalm 107 pictures the redeemed gathering from the east and from the west and from the north and from the south. This song of praise raised as the people of Israel were coming back from a time of exile is recast in Luke's Gospel. Here the invitation to the gospel is laced with words of warning. Jesus is asked, "Lord, will only a few be saved?" Jesus responds that the invitation comes with a need for decision. One must strive to enter the door before it is closed, for it is not enough simply to say that we ate and drank together! Eating and drinking in God's kingdom are grounded in a shared commitment to follow God's way.

Jesus offers a new vision of God's kingdom only after the pronouncement of judgment on those who failed to respond. In God's new reign, people will come. And those who were last will be first. This prophetic word challenges all those who are invited to the table. On the one hand, come! All are welcome to hear the good news and respond to God's invitation. And yet, coming to the table requires change in our lives and a radical reordering of our expectations about who is welcome at this meal.

What Does It Look Like?

At a leadership training event I attended, one of our speakers talked about the work of starting a new congregation in a large urban area.[4] Those involved in the planning identified several key practices that all new members agreed to share. Some were typical spiritual disciplines: prayer, reading of Scripture, sharing of financial resources. I was struck by one practice in particular. The group agreed that at some time during each month, each person would invite a neighbor to dinner. The purpose of the meal was not proselytizing. It was simply to get to know one's own neighbors around a table. At first, he reported, it seemed an easy assignment. Find neighbors you would like to get to know and then invite them over for dinner. After a few months, though, he quickly became weary of the practice. He began to dread finding another stranger and inviting that person into his home to share a meal. That is when he began to realize what this practice actually involves. Sharing a meal with strangers can be awkward and uncomfortable. And yet, breaking bread together creates connections and bonds between people who might otherwise never meet.

This is precisely what the church's invitation to the table is all about: creating a space where we are invited to meet with strangers and friends. Responding to this invitation is a first step toward acting on Jesus's words of warning and hope. The invitation to the table itself presents an opportunity for transformation as it casts judgment on our expectation to control who belongs in the community. In the Gospels, Jesus's table practices defy the expectations of those in the religious community who believe the invitation to eat requires both hosts and guests to follow rigid rules. In place of regulations comes an openness to welcome others to the table and to share life with our neighbors.

However, surprises lie in store for those who stagger in, as well as for those who presume special treatment. The last will be at the front of the line, and the first will be bringing up the rear. Our images of table etiquette are challenged and expanded by this reversal of fortunes. The invitation to the table carries with it a sense of judgment that pushes us to look around our worship spaces to see who is there and to reflect on who is absent. When our congregations are made up solely of people who look like us and think like us, then we fall short of the biblical vision of people coming from all corners of the earth to share this meal together. The geographical directions represent one important form of diversity to work toward in our faith communities. Couched in this language are other sorts of differences that often separate us. Jesus's words of judgment in the Gospel of Luke strike at the sense of entitlement that some bring to the assembly. Of course, we expect to find a place at the table for ourselves!

The invitation to the table can become a simple routine that is easily overlooked. Yet in certain moments it retains a power to shape and transform us and enlarge the circles of people in our lives. In those times and places where our experiences of table hospitality are challenged, then our notions about who is invited are radically expanded.

In a small courtyard outside a modest home in the sprawling city of Managua, Nicaragua, a few of us arrived to visit a new house church. Stacks of white plastic patio chairs were placed in rows. A basket and a Bible rested atop a folding table near the front of the space. During the service, an elder brought forward a round tin tray. On it was half a coconut shell filled with small packets of crackers and small plastic cups of homemade wine. The worship leader spoke briefly about the importance of communion, and then he looked to us as the guests and invited us to offer words and to pray. I stood up and offered brief words of gratitude for the generous invitation to share this experience. Together, in Spanish and English we shared words of Scripture that welcomed friends and strangers at this table to share simple gifts of wheat and grape.

During the closing hymn, our Nicaraguan hosts quickly cleared the folding table and brought out trays of cookies and cups of strong, hot coffee. We gathered around the table again for conversation and sharing. The table had brought us together and given us a common experience. Here worship intersects with life. The pattern that began in communion grew to a lively conversation between neighbors and strangers.

Whether it is a folding table on a patio or an ornate marble slab, Christians call this furniture the Lord's table. What do we mean by referring to it as "the Lord's table"? We bring food and drink to it, and we create rules and restrictions about who can lead the prayers and even about who can come to eat and drink. These rules, which are not included in Scripture, reflect the sensibilities of various Christian gatherings with their own distinct cultural practices and theological inclinations.

Yet we continue to call it the Lord's table. One could dismiss it as an old, quaint way of speaking in church (of which there are many examples). I would like to believe that this pattern of speech preserves a basic understanding that despite our attempts to control who gathers around this table, it does not belong to us. For those newcomers and strangers who find their way through our church doors, this table, the Lord's table, is a place where all are welcome to come and eat—sometimes in spite of the obstacles we put in the way. For as the language of the liturgy claims, the invitation comes not just from the one who is presiding. The invitation to eat, drink, and share life together comes from the Spirit of the risen Christ, who meets us and welcomes us as we gather around this table. This invitation begins with bread and wine but quickly leads to experiences of sharing our lives with those who gather at table with us.

Welcome Words

Presider:	The Lord be with you.
Congregation:	*And also with you.*
Presider:	Lift up your hearts.
Congregation:	*We lift them to the Lord.*
Presider:	Let us give thanks to the Lord our God.
Congregation:	*It is right to give our thanks and praise.*

This exchange between presider and congregation highlights the themes of mutual hospitality at the table. As a greeting and as a word of blessing, the words "the Lord be with you" hearken to an ancient model.[5] Their importance is grounded in the practice of extending God's blessing to all those around us. In worship services, where we are surrounded by family, friends, and strangers, these words take on added significance. Together, we offer a prayer for God's presence to surround all who have gathered for this communion meal. In and through these simple and ancient words, we extend God's blessing to one another.

Similarly, the invitation to lift up our hearts calls us as a community to discover God's presence in our midst. Setting aside distractions, we turn our attention to God. The words "Lift up your hearts" urge us to concentrate on the primary purpose of this gathering and this meal, which is to cultivate a sense of thanksgiving. The exchange here captures the spirit of the apostle Paul's words in Colossians 3: "So if you have been raised with Christ, seek the things that are above, where Christ is, seated at the right hand of God."[6]

Finally, we are called to give God thanks. Surrounded by the gift of one another, encouraged to ground our thoughts and actions in the presence of Christ, we offer our prayer of gratitude to God. This act embodies the very essence of the table prayer (for the word *eucharist* simply means "thanksgiving"). This simple exchange of words between presider and congregation provides the framework and foundation for the entire meal. Our daily lives are shaped by extending God's blessing to all, focusing on Christ's presence, and offering thanks. The invitation to the table urges us beyond our notions of friendship toward a model that is grounded in our baptism. As God's new family, we gather with all who come as followers of Jesus. In thanksgiving for God's grace, we extend our hands and offer words of blessing to one another.

Hymn for Reflection

I come with joy, a child of God,
Forgiven, loved and free,
The life of Jesus to recall,
In love laid down for me.

I come with Christians far and near
To find, as all are fed,
The new community of love
In Christ's communion bread.

As Christ breaks bread, and bids us share,
Each proud division ends.
The love that made us, makes us one,
And strangers now are friends.

The Spirit of the risen Christ,
Unseen, but ever near,
Is in such friendship better known,
Alive among us here.

Together met, together bound
By all that God has done,
We'll go with joy, to give the world
The love that makes us one.[7]

Questions for Discussion

1. In considering the relationship between table practice and hospitality, reflect on the Jewish observance of Passover, in which an empty chair and place setting are provided for the hoped-for return of the prophet Elijah. A door is left ajar and a window opened to provide him entry. What does this practice say about hospitality and meals?

2. What do you think of the understanding of friendship presented here, that friends are not simply "whom we like, with whom we agree, or even with whom we share common interests"? How do friends, relatives, fellow church members, and strangers form community, and what role does the Lord's Supper play in this process?

3. Describe your experiences of communion in light of joy or mourning. What has been most common? What has been most powerful?

4. Recite or sing together the Hymn for Reflection on pages 60–61. How do these words reflect on the chapter you have just read or the conversation you have shared? The words of this hymn speak of coming, alone and together, into Christ's presence in communion bread, and how that supper changes our relationship with one another and with Jesus himself. Has a common meal ever had the effect of breaking down divisions in your experience? Can you imagine how a holy meal can have that result among you, your congregation, and God?

CHAPTER 5

Discovering God and Finding Our Own Identity

Blessed are you, gracious God,
Creator of light, Giver of all life, Source of love.
Your song of wisdom rang out before the world began;
Your ancient love still touches us and stirs within us.[1]

A small assembly gathered near the beach on a warm fall morning. Following a brief sermon, the minister invited us to gather around a large picnic table. Orange and yellow leaves drifted down from the trees and fell around us as a breeze blew gently across the waters of Puget Sound. As the minister quietly spoke, her words hung in the air. "Blessed are you, gracious God, creator of this good earth. You are the fountain of all life and source of all goodness."[2] As the sun shone down upon us, we were bathed in the beauty of God's splendor.

In the invitation to the table, the presiding minister welcomes us to take our place as the assembly gathers around the central elements of Word, water, bread, and wine (these things that shape our practices of preaching, baptism, and communion). This act of gathering leads to prayer that connects us to the earth as God's creation, to those who have gone before us witnessing to God's goodness and grace, and to a vision of life centered in wholeness and holiness.

Becoming Grounded

The communion prayer starts by acknowledging God and thanking God for the goodness of creation. While different denominations debate whether Christ's presence in the communion elements is best understood as "real" or "spiritual," the prayer begins firmly grounded on earth. The minister, a flesh-and-blood human being, raises her arms and calls out to God. She stands firmly planted on the ground, dressed in a white robe, calling out in a clear voice and expressing thanks to God for creating the world and placing us in it to care for and nurture the goodness of creation. In front of her is a table made of wood. On it is a clay pitcher, chalice, and plate. Soon bread will be broken and wine or juice poured.

This stuff, these earthly things of creation, are at the center of the community's prayer of thanksgiving. Often we rush past these things and want to get to the "true meaning" of them. Yet, here we are, part of the creation, giving thanks to God. Leading from the table is a way of living out the poetic vision of Psalm 148. For the psalmist, all of creation joins together to praise the Lord. The sun, moon, stars, and highest heavens offer their joyous praise. The earth, sea monsters, fire, hail, snow, frost, and stormy wind praise the Creator. Mountains and hills, trees, and all sorts of animals join in the chorus. All people, powerful and humble, young and old, give glory and thanksgiving to God.

This praise and joy infuse the gathering at the table so that it becomes a joyous feast of the people of God. Prayer at the table is firmly grounded in the goodness of the creation that God makes and sustains. The prayer also underscores the biblical witness that God longs and works for creation to experience wholeness. This framework provides a foundation for Christian engagement in caring for the earth. Coming to the table is a first step toward reorienting our lives and practices. We are all increasingly aware of the crisis of global warming. In the face of predictions of immanent catastrophe, it is easy for us to become paralyzed. Here at the table, guided by our thanksgiving for God's good gifts of creation, our eyes are opened to our responsibility of preserving the earth.

This prayer presents the earth as a beautiful canvas that elicits admiration and points to the inherent goodness of God's work. Like a great piece of art that we long to see and to share with others, the work of maintaining and caring for the earth requires attention and commitment. The prayer at the table places us together within all of creation and calls us to join our voices in praise. Rather than draw us inward with our eyes tightly closed in search of some private space, this prayer links us with one another and with the goodness of the earth that surrounds us. United around the table with our neighbors and these gifts of bread and wine, we join our voices in praising God.

Prayer at the table offers a vision of life in harmony with our neighbors and with all creation. The prayer serves to guide and challenge the choices we make each day. How do we, through the groceries we buy and the food we eat each day, support a sustainable future for the environment? Does our acquisition and consumption of things provide a way of life that can last from generation to generation? Are we caring for the earth so that it will continue to sing out in praise to the Creator?

Two years ago, my wife and I bought a townhouse. The small courtyard out back had borders of ornamental grass and lots of barkdust (mulch). It was neat and tidy with no weeds in sight. The previous owners had maintained this sense of order by constant application of toxic chemicals to limit any growth other than the ornamental grass. We are gradually reclaiming the land by removing the barkdust and turning the soil as we add nutrients back into the earth. Slowly but surely, the earth is coming back to life. Birds that were never sighted in our yard have come back to scratch in the soil. A small vegetable garden is growing on one side of the yard. There are certainly weeds to pull and work to do, but now when we look out our bedroom window we see the gifts of creation and the goodness of the earth. As flowers blossom and the bean plants climb up the tall wooden stakes, we give thanks for the sun and rain that God provides. Each day the patch of ground helps us connect to the goodness of creation. Through this awareness we give thanks for the gift of life. By this practice our lives are shaped and molded as we discover God's blessings and presence that surround us.

Small steps toward caring for the earth can begin as we pay close attention to the prayer at the table. This prayer is not a utopian vision for a different world. Nor does it deny the immense work that needs to be done in our world. The communion prayer itself holds out images of the goodness of creation while recognizing its brokenness. Surprisingly, the language of the prayer at table provides us with a balanced portrait of the hope and challenges that we and all creation face. Yes, God created us and all the world to live in peace and harmony. However, we turned away from lives grounded in thanksgiving and praise. The prayer goes on to proclaim that God does not turn away from us and continues to call us back to lives of faithfulness, justice, and reconciliation.

Here the eucharistic prayer models a significant interconnection between God and all creation. In spite of humanity's rebellion and selfishness, God continues to reach out and claim us as sons and daughters. Thus, the prayer invites us to care for the earth as part of God's faithful covenant working to reconcile all creation. Coming to the table is a first step in responding to the invitation to find our place in God's covenant. Effective leaders name specific places where members of the community can make a difference. Each Saturday, a friend of mine goes to a school in a distressed neighborhood to pick up the trash that litters the playground. This faithful witness led neighborhood volunteers to join her, providing a clean and safe place for children to play.

This theme of joining and caring for creation is particularly prominent in an "Altar Garden Liturgy" for eucharistic services by Philip Newell, a Church of Scotland minister and leader of Celtic spirituality. The prayer recognizes the beauty of the world around us and invites us to join in a song of praise.

> With the whole realm of nature around us,
> with earth, sea and sky we sing to you:
> with angels of light who envelop us,
> and with saints of heaven and earth,
> we join in the song of your never ending greatness.[3]

Eucharistic prayers that are grounded in the goodness of creation provide a framework for calling Christians to ecological awareness and care for the earth. The language of the prayer itself pushes us to tend to creation so that its witness to God's glory is preserved. Good bread we taste and good wine we share are signs of God's blessing on our earth. Through God's faithfulness, the sun, rain, and soil produce crops that nourish us. Thanksgiving for these basic elements of God's creation is at the center of the communion prayer.

Family Connections

The prayer remembers and names those who precede us: our ancestors, who model ways to reorient our lives in thanksgiving and praise. Sarah and Abraham, Moses and Miriam, Esther, Ruth, and David all serve as examples of those who testified to God's love for us.[4] One prayer in particular holds up these biblical models of faith while noting that "even they turned away from you and forgot about you, as we do too."[5]

The prayer at table pictures the beauty of the world and calls us to reorient our lives so that this glory may become a reality for us. At the same time, it acknowledges how often we fail to live out this vision. By recalling those members of our faith family (part of the roll call of saints) whose lives point towards wholeness, we are challenged to rediscover our identity as sons and daughters of God in light of our baptism. The story that unfolds in the communion prayer begins with the goodness of creation while acknowledging our failures to live in harmony and justice with one another and with the whole earth. While recognizing our fallenness, it points to the continued desire and work of God to reclaim us and all of creation. When we turned away from God and pursued our own interests, God did not turn from us but continued to reach out to us. Prophets like Jeremiah and Amos call us to leave behind our selfish commitments to greed and exploitation of our neighbors. These prophets call us back to the covenant that God has established with all of creation.

At the table, this message of judgment and redemption is grounded ultimately in the life of Jesus Christ. As part of God's covenant with the Hebrew people and in continuity with the prophetic witness, Jesus comes to testify to God's ongoing commitment to restoring our relationships with God, with one another, and with all of creation.

The prayer at the table tells the truth about our past when it speaks of our infidelity. Yet it also holds up a vision of hope of all creation singing praise to God. This hope grows out of the waters of baptism, where God recreates a new family. At the table, the communion prayer joins with the baptismal prayer as we experience a new family that is born of water and not simply of blood ties. Like the prayer at the font, the prayer at the table calls out the names of our family members who have gone before us: Noah, Moses, and the children of Israel. Around the table, this new family gathers to share this meal and to live out this vision of a new way of life. As at our own family gatherings, the table prayer retells the stories of those who have gone before us. These narratives provide a broader sense of our family identity and kinship.

Learning to claim these family connections is a part of making the communion prayer a part of our lives. At the end of the semester, our class gathered for a meal in our home. It had been a challenging class. We had read difficult texts together and had worked hard at understanding the role that rituals play in our lives. I decided to try a new way to celebrate our accomplishments as a class. I moved the table and chairs out of the dining room and put the coffee table in their place. We gathered up pillows from around the house and placed them on the floor around it. I hired a friend of ours to cater a Mediterranean meal. Once the students had all arrived, we gathered in a circle for prayer. We gave thanks for God's goodness to us as a class and asked God's blessings on a pitcher of water that I held in my hands. Then two of us took the water, a bowl, and a towel to each person and washed each one's hands in preparation for the meal we were about to share.

We took our places on the floor around the low table, and for the next three hours we slowly savored a wonderful meal. During the time together, we named our thanksgivings for the opportunity to read and study together. We gave thanks for authors whose works had stretched our minds and imaginations. We grounded our identity as a class in the work of scholars who had helped us see the world in new ways. In this process, our class deepened our ties with one another even as we recognized ways in which we were connected to a much larger community. These words and acts, done around the table, parallel ways in which the eucharistic prayer grounds our identities as followers of Jesus Christ in the biblical story that connects us with a family that has gone before us.

This experience of naming those who have shared and modeled the faith to us is a way of reclaiming the power of personal testimony. In a recent eucharistic prayer, Gail Ramshaw, a Lutheran theologian, has provided an outline that allows for improvisation in parts of the prayer. Here, biblical characters from the readings of the day take their place in calling us to the table.

> We praise you for your covenant people,
> for Moses and Miriam and Aaron,
> (here may be added three more Old Testament figures.)[6]

One of the great strengths of this kind of prayer is that it allows those who are praying to add references from the Scripture readings for the day. The family tree grows out of the scriptural witness that includes the readings for the day as we gather around the table.

Moving towards Wholeness

The prayer at the table follows an intrinsic progression: our grounding as part of God's creation leads to cultivating a deeper sense of care for the earth; our acknowledgment of those who have gone before us opens our eyes to those around us who model faithful service. These movements in the prayer are linked to a vision of life that is whole. The prayer places us in relationship to the earth and to one another so that we may discover and claim our identity as children of God.

For Christians who gather around the table, this movement toward wholeness is possible only as we acknowledge our dependence on God who is known to us in Jesus Christ. Christ represents the culmination of creation and is a full expression of God's commitment to the world. In the context of the communion prayer, Jesus's life, death, and resurrection testify to God's ongoing redemptive work, which calls all men and women to respond to God's love. In the fullness of time, Jesus comes to proclaim and embody God's grace, which leads us from brokenness to wholeness. In Christ, we discover the depth and commitment of God's love of us and of this world.

Recent work on baptism expands the vision and experience of baptism to include preparation for baptism as well as growth into our baptismal vows. The ancient model of the catechumenate (a period of study) is a way to prepare and gauge readiness for baptism, celebrate the richness of baptism, and explore ways that our gifts and understanding of vocation are grounded in baptism. Baptism is not just a moment in time but a lifelong journey of the faith. In a similar way, the prayer at the table traces the movement of God's grace throughout time as it begins in creation, unfolds through the biblical witness, culminates in Jesus Christ, and extends to include us in this gathering. We are not the initiators of this movement. Instead we are invited to join a movement that extends through time and creation. Thus, the words of the prayer at table invite us to join our voices with those of all time and of every place who forever sing to the glory of God.

The traditional response that is sung in the communion prayer is the Sanctus.

> Holy, holy, holy Lord,
> God of power and might,
> heaven and earth are full of your glory.
> Hosanna in the highest.
> Blessed is the one who comes in the name of the Lord.
> Hosanna in the highest.

This song comes from Scripture itself and is a vision of God's glory. In the sixth chapter of Isaiah, the prophet recalls seeing

God's glory and grandeur. In this vision, Isaiah is transported to the throne of God and is surrounded by angels who call out to one another in praise of God's holiness. This dramatic rendering of God's transcendence and majesty was central to the prophetic witness of God's presence. Awe and adoration are the marks of one who captures a glimpse of God. Isaiah places this portrait of his call as a prophet in the context of his vision of God's grandeur. In response to his encounter with the divine, Isaiah offers himself as a witness to the children of Israel.[7]

The song of adoration of the angels in Isaiah became part of the prayers of faithful Jewish people. The words of Psalm 118:26 ("Blessed is the one who comes in the name of the Lord") were added to the song of the angels to highlight the call that sends us out in God's name. The familiar words of this psalm were already a thanksgiving hymn used in the prayers at the temple. We do not know when and where the eucharistic Sanctus was compiled, but some scholars believe that the conflation of these two prayers began in Jewish synagogues and later came to be part of the regular meal prayers of Jewish families.[8] In the synagogue the prayers of thanksgiving began with a blessing for creation and led to a blessing for God's redemptive work. The synagogue prayers ended with a cry for God's promises to be fulfilled. Over time, meal prayers in the home took this same shape, with a prayer of thanksgiving for creation, a prayer of gratitude for redemption, and a prayer of intercession for the coming of God's reign. Here thanksgiving for God's faithfulness is connected with our identity as members of the covenant and a plea for God to bring salvation and healing to the world around us. These ancient Jewish prayers point to a long-standing practice of linking prayers in the worship space with the table prayers of the faithful.

In New Testament times, early Jewish Christians continued to use prayers that they learned in the synagogue and temple. Acts 2 reports that the apostles and other followers of Jesus devoted themselves to "the prayers" and continued to spend much time together in the temple. It seems likely that this ancient form of table prayer became a basic piece of the prayer of thanksgiving as followers of Jesus gathered around the table to break bread and share the cup.

Today when Christians join to sing the Sanctus, we are united in this ancient witness to God's faithfulness and goodness. These words sum up the opening stanza of the table prayer as we sing of God's blessing and goodness in creation and redemption. At the same time, the text witnesses to Christ's incarnation and to our continual longing for the healing and culmination of all creation.

When we sing the Sanctus, we often think particularly of Jesus's triumphal entry into Jerusalem. The Gospels report that crowds of people lined the way, laid their cloaks on the path, and waved palms as Jesus rode into the city on a donkey. The crowds along the way called out the words of Psalm 118:26: "Hosanna to the Son of David! Blessed is the one who comes in the name of the Lord! Hosanna in the highest heaven" (Matt. 21:9). Since this psalm was sung as part of the Passover celebration, it was already on the lips of those gathering to celebrate this festival. Its location as part of the procession for the Passover in Jerusalem in the Gospels underscores the messianic expectations that Jesus will restore the Davidic kingdom and lead Israel into a time of prosperity.

A rabbi in Tacoma, Washington, invited members of his faith community to offer a traditional prayer of thanksgiving, "Blessed are you, O God, creator of the universe," every time they caught a glimpse of Mount Rainier. This way of praying helps frame the way that we see the world. Slowly it builds a deeper appreciation for creation and for our responsibility in caring for it so that it may continue to serve as a testimony to the Creator's presence. As these words of ancient prayers become a part of our vocabulary, we accept a responsibility to protect the beauty of the world around us and to work for the healing of our planet.

While the associations of this song of thanksgiving with a particular time in the life of Jesus are significant, reclaiming the witness of Isaiah's vision of God's majesty helps us see the awesome presence of God in the beauty of creation. Heaven and earth are indeed full of God's glory. We sing with thankful hearts for the goodness of creation. Inspired by this witness, our eyes are opened to see the world as God's magnificent canvas. Prayer calls us to action.

Moving Time

In the eucharistic prayer, verb tenses shift around. Creation is not simply an event in the distant past. Even when past tenses are used ("You created us in your image"), the prayer is not about events that simply happened long ago. The past is no longer discrete or cut off from the future. Likewise, the future is not simply far off in the distance. In the prayer at the table, verb tenses collapse into this present moment. At the table, time is fluid. The telling of the past recapitulates events and allows them to be present among us. The longing for the future intersects with the possibility that in some way the future is present right now. The present moment around the table opens the door to the witnesses from the past and to God's vision of a new heaven and earth.

The Sanctus shares the fluid quality of time in the communion prayer. Our song of God's holiness in this time and place joins the song of other faithful worshipers. It also leads us into the future. As we sing a blessing of the One who comes in the name of the Lord, we are not only taken to the events of Jesus's entry into Jerusalem but are also invited to join with all those who come in the name of the Lord. Here, our longing for the fulfillment of God's promises is united with the longing of those who have sung throughout history. At the same time, these words color the way that we look at those who are working for the establishment of peace and justice as a part of God's coming reign. Christ's life is a pattern for us to follow. Because we are made the beloved children of God in baptism, the words of the Sanctus offer a blessing on our own lives.

The Sanctus points to ways to reclaim the process of sanctification in our lives. Our Christian growth toward holiness is placed in the context of our awareness of God's glory and transcendence and our service to our neighbor as we become those who come in the name of the Lord. Sanctification is the process of living into the vision offered in the prayer. As we serve one another and those around us in the name of the Lord, we find that our lives become holy signs of God's presence in our world. We become blessed as we participate in the redemptive work of God in the world.

As we live out of this language and our lives are shaped by these words, then we find ourselves in the middle of this prayer. As we respond to the needs in the world around us, then we discover that the words of the prayer are addressed to us. We become the ones who are blessed to come in the name of the Lord.

Growing into Grace

This opening stanza of the communion prayer paints a picture of the world around us and of our place within it. As does God's good gift of creation, the prayer proclaims the continued presence of God in the world. The prayer recalls the ancestors of our faith who have worked, taught, and acted to hold up God's faithful covenant with Israel and with the church. And the prayer invites us to find ways to participate and live into this vision of a renewed heaven and earth. As we sing out in thanksgiving for God's glory and grace, we are called to participate in the healing of our lives, our relationships, and the world around us. These steps toward holiness, of growing into grace, are part of the journey that the communion prayer invites us on. It is a journey led by the risen Christ, on which we hold up the names of saints who have gone before us and are surrounded by brothers and sisters in Christ as we join together in God's redemptive work in our world.

Hymn for Reflection

For the fruit of all creation,
Thanks be to God.
For the gifts to every nation,
Thanks be to God.
For the plowing, sowing, reaping,
Silent growth while we are sleeping,
Future needs in earth's safekeeping,
Thanks be to God.

In the just reward of labor,
God's will be done.
In the help we give our neighbor,
God's will be done.
In our worldwide task of caring
For the hungry and despairing,
In the harvests we are sharing,
God's will be done.

For the harvests of the spirit,
Thanks be to God.
For the good we all inherit,
Thanks be to God.
For the wonders that astound us,
For the truths that still confound,
Most of all that love has found us,
Thanks be to God.[9]

Questions for Discussion

1. Think about family dinners you have attended recently or in the past. Where did people sit, and how did this express the relationships at the table? Who was the host, who prepared the food, and how did their places at the table reflect that? How does this arrangement relate to the Lord's Table?

2. As Christians, why is it important that the communion prayer "begins firmly grounded on earth"? How do the elements of bread and cup connect us to earth, to heaven, and from earth *to* heaven? What does this understanding say about "our responsibility of preserving the earth"?

3. Gardening is suggested as a small step of caring for the earth, one that helps us pay attention to the prayer and the Lord's Table. What other simple actions in daily life can provide connections to God's presence in and around us?

4. We read that "the prayer at the table calls out the names of our family members who have gone before us." Take a moment to think of those who have greatly influenced your faith, including family members, Sunday school teachers, pastors, and friends. What does it mean to you to know that you are with those saints who have gone before us?

5. Recite or sing together the Hymn for Reflection on pages 74–75. How do these words reflect on the chapter you have just read or the conversation you have shared? The famous mystic Meister Eckhart wrote, "If the only prayer we say is 'thank you' that is enough." In this hymn we thank God for creation and for congregation. Is there a connection here? In the final stanza, thanksgiving is sung for "wonders that astound us, for the truths that still confound us" and for God's love that is always with us. What do you think is the relationship between this challenge and this promise?

CHAPTER 6

Encountering Christ and Offering Ourselves

I appeal to you therefore, brothers and sisters, by the mercies of God, to present your bodies as a living sacrifice, holy and acceptable to God, which is your reasonable service.[1]

On a Wednesday evening, about twenty of us gathered in a small chapel next to the large sanctuary in a downtown church. An older minister led the service with a brief reflection on the Gospel reading for the day and a prayer at the communion table that ended in an invitation to commit ourselves to following Christ. After communion, the minister stood behind the table and announced that immediately after the service we would walk together to join others who were gathered at city hall to speak out against the production of nuclear missiles at a factory in our community. The plant's history of pouring toxic chemicals into groundwater had been overlooked by those eager to support high-paying jobs at all costs. It was time to speak out, announced the minister, to move from the safety of the chapel and work for change in our neighborhood.

From Creation to Christ

In the previous chapter, we observed the movement in the eucharistic prayer that opens with God's faithful presence in creation and leads up to the birth of Jesus. The end of this section of the communion prayer foreshadows the focus on Christ as the culmination of creation before inviting the assembly to join in the Sanctus. This transition leads to the heart of the prayer, which is grounded in the life, ministry, death, and resurrection of Jesus Christ.

Throughout the history of the church, significant debates have been waged over divergent theological perspectives on Christ's presence at the table. It is not the purpose of this chapter to plow through these often obscure points of contention one more time. Instead, our attention is focused on the role of Jesus as model for our lives and as the focal point of the communion prayer. In framing the discussion in these terms, we hope to avoid the deep level of debates that often divide the church. While areas of historical conflict cannot be avoided altogether, a brief discussion of terms and distinctions between different Christian traditions will lead to a more thorough exploration of the christological center of communion prayer. Our guiding focus will be on the purpose of eucharistic prayer.

In late medieval times, the conversations on this topic led to historic divisions in the church. At the center of the Reformation debate was a reexamination of notions of sacrifice in the mass. Martin Luther and others leaders highly criticized the sacrificial imagery associated with the medieval mass. In Geneva, John Calvin reoriented communion practices by moving the altar from the front wall of the sanctuary into the middle of the sanctuary and referring to it as a table. The significance of this relocation was to distance the acts at the table from the idea that the mass was a re-sacrifice of Christ. In Zurich, Ulrich Zwingli went even further by sending the elements into the congregation so that worshipers would not continue to approach the table as they did in the mass.

These debates often included crass mischaracterizations of the opponent's position. On the one hand, Protestants' inflammatory attacks on the description of graphic resacrificing of Christ by Roman Catholic priests failed to recognize a more nuanced view held by many within the Catholic Church. Likewise, Roman Catholics often had difficulty accepting more qualified notions of the events taking place at the table. Lost in this struggle was the large area of agreement among many of the participants that the entire sacramental act, including the prayer of thanksgiving, was grounded in the story of Jesus Christ.

Centering on Christ

We have already explored some of the implications of Jesus's own table practices for a broader perspective of our celebration of the Lord's Supper. There is growing awareness among liturgical scholars that the entirety of the Gospels provides insight into the church's development of sacramental practices. Thus, meals during Jesus's public ministry and following his resurrection offer significant insights on ways for us to gather to break bread and share the cup in thanksgiving as we re-member Jesus Christ.[2] Focusing the conversation around the centrality of Christ in our communion practices allows us to emphasize the primary area of agreements among denominations rather than to replay theological debates.

In the very structure of the communion prayer itself, Jesus Christ is central. After recognizing creation as an expression of God's glory and remembering God's faithfulness in sending prophets to call God's people back to the covenant, the prayer turns to Jesus. The phrase "in the fullness of time" parallels the gospel understanding of a *kairos*, the right time. At the proper time or in just the right moment, Jesus displays God's redemptive work in our world.

This central part of the prayer at table follows the outline of Jesus's birth, ministry, death, and resurrection. As a summary of Jesus's life, the prayer becomes a form of gospel proclamation in its own right. Rather than simply rush to the cross and present a theological interpretation of atonement,[3] prayers from the table should point to the incarnational witness of Jesus's life. Born of Mary, Jesus lives as God's grace among us.

While theologians often speak of the integral connection between baptism and communion (with coming to the table and receiving communion as a way of renewing our baptismal vows), it seems odd that mention of Jesus's baptism is rarely found in communion prayers. One exception is the communion prayer in the *Book of Common Worship* for the Sunday of the Baptism of the Lord. Here, the prayer includes these words:

> Baptized in Jordan's waters,
> Jesus took his place with sinners
> and your voice proclaimed him your beloved."[4]

This language not only reinforces basic baptismal imagery but also provides a vision of Jesus's solidarity with all who come to both font and table in response to God's invitation. The wording also provides a theological foundation for the church's declaration that in baptism all of us are declared beloved children of God. As Jesus was declared as God's beloved son in the waters of baptism, so too in our baptism we are declared beloved children of God. In this sense, the portrait of solidarity in the words of this communion prayer shows Jesus's identification with us as sinners in his baptism and our identification with Christ in God's acceptance of us as sons and daughters in our baptism.

Prayers that include Jesus's baptism as a defining moment at the onset of his public ministry provide a foundation for us to discover this integral connection between our baptism and our own callings as Christians. As Jesus's baptism leads to engagement in public ministry, so too our own baptisms mark the beginning of discernment about our gifts and callings as disciples of Jesus Christ.[5] Thus, communion prayers that explicitly recall Jesus's baptism provide direct links to broaden our theological vocabulary and baptismal understanding.

Life and Death at the Crossroads

Following this recounting of Jesus's birth and baptism, the prayer at the table turns to his public ministry. His teaching and healing made God's reign visible. In solidarity with the poor, he lived a simple life. He welcomed strangers and broke bread with sinners and outcasts. He proclaimed the good news of the kingdom of God to all people. When a brief outline of Jesus's life is included, the prayer offers a more holistic vision of ways we can follow in Christ's footsteps.

Even the terms *Lord's Table* and *Lord's Supper* point to Christ as the primary reason for gathering at the table. Thus, it is important for communion prayers to include Jesus's birth, baptism, public ministry of healing, teaching, welcoming, and judging. Jesus's public ministry and confrontation with religious and political powers, the prayers remind us, prompted the events that led to Jesus's death in Jerusalem. Communion prayers should provide a context for the cross as a way of speaking of Christ's crucifixion and as a way to point to the cost of discipleship today.

There is a decided lack of agreement among and even within denominations about how to describe Jesus's ministry in the communion prayer. In some prayers, the language about Jesus focuses on the cross as a source of salvation. Other prayers (and particularly some of the more recent ones) present an outline of Jesus's life, ministry, death, and resurrection. The purpose in these broader prayers is not to diminish the place of the cross. Among all Christians, the cross stands as the basic symbol of God's presence in the midst of human pain and suffering. All faithful accounts of Jesus include the suffering endured by Jesus on the cross. The issue is whether communion prayers that focus on a specific theological interpretation of the doctrine of atonement, such as substitutionary atonement, do justice to the portrait of Jesus presented in the Gospels.

When the language of the communion prayer moves beyond the cross and summarizes the life of Jesus, *then* it proclaims the gospel to the entire assembly. It also foreshadows a basic outline of Christian life. When leaders offer prayers that point to the basic components of Jesus's ministry and our Christian callings, then they clearly identify Christian commitment to living in solidarity with the poor, feeding the hungry, clothing the naked, visiting the imprisoned, and tending to the sick and neglected.

The communion prayer still points to the reality of sacrifice that is a part of Christian discipleship. Jesus's vision of God's reign is rejected by authorities in Jerusalem and leads to Jesus's suffering and death. In this sense, nearly all forms of communion prayer stress the cross as evidence of the conflict between Jesus and the established religious and political powers. At this point, the prayer serves as a model and also as a warning about the high cost of discipleship for those who follow in Jesus's steps.

Communion prayers that present the gospel in brief offer testimony to Jesus's faithful dependence on God. This testimony serves as a road map to those who wish to follow Christ's example. The eucharistic prayer presents the life of Jesus as a pattern of service and sacrifice to lay alongside our lives. Christ's life serves as an icon or image for our lives. What portrait of Jesus is presented in the communion prayer? If the prayer only recounts the sacrificial death of Jesus, then we are left with virtually no pattern for our own lives. Since it is unlikely that we will be persecuted, let alone martyred for our faith, focusing solely on the cross in this section of the communion prayers fails to provide us with a template for our lives. Thus, when the primary image is of Jesus's sacrificial death, we are separated from Jesus's life of teaching, preaching, and healing rather than drawn into it. Communion prayers that present a wider collage of Jesus's life guide us to live as followers of Jesus Christ.

For example, to mention Jesus's care for the poor is to reassert the basic biblical claim that God has a particular interest in the plight of the poor. The prayer invites us to identify and respond to the needs of the poor as we live in light of the Jesus story. To speak of Jesus's acts of healing and exorcism is to call those who come to the table to tend to the needs of the sick and to fight the forces of oppression in our society. To recall that Jesus ate with sinners and outcasts is to challenge us to share our food with those whom we sometimes judge or ignore. It is in this broader sketch of Jesus's life that the power of the cross finds its place, for here the cross stands as testimony to Jesus's solidarity with all those who are forgotten, abused, and condemned. In the communion prayer, the cross and Jesus's suffering serve as a warning that faithful discipleship exacts a cost. Like Jesus's words to his first disciples about the high price of following him, the communion prayer reminds us that while God's grace is freely offered, lives of service will require us to make sacrifices. In the midst of this warning, the communion prayer also offers hope. Christ's resurrection assures us that God will continue to breathe new life into our world, our communities, and ourselves. In the process depicted by the apostle Paul, as I die to self, Christ lives in me (Gal. 2:20). Resurrection is not simply a theological event connected with Jesus's life; it is God's promise to all believers that in the midst of death, we will receive new life.

Oblation and Obligation

Our conversation leads to a broader examination of the role of sacrifice and offering in the communion prayer. Eucharistic prayers across denominational differences continue to rely heavily on sacrificial imagery. In its basic form, the question of sacrifice can be put this way: what is being offered at the communion table? Church traditions have answered this question in drastically different ways. Some have argued that communion is the re-presentation of the physical body of Christ, while others have suggested that the primary role of the communion prayer is to remind us of the sacrifice Jesus made long ago. An alternative proposal is to view the congregation's praise and thanksgiving as an offering and sacrifice.[6] A strength of this perspective is that it affirms the assembly's active participation in the prayer. While there are positive elements to this understanding, it fails to demonstrate how the assembly's prayer of thanksgiving is actually a sacrifice.[7]

Rather than rehash the discussion that has historically divided the church, let us focus on a basic biblical claim that can unite us as we gather at the table. In Romans 12:1, the apostle Paul urges us to come before God and offer our own lives: "I appeal to you therefore, brothers and sisters, by the mercies of God, to present your bodies as a living sacrifice, holy and acceptable to God, which is your spiritual [reasonable] worship."

Instead of engaging in endless debate about theological interpretations of the eucharistic prayer, Paul is inviting us to understand ourselves as the offering that is presented to God. Coming to the table and receiving God's grace and blessing constitute our primary act of worship. We present ourselves as a living sacrifice so that our work is no longer self-serving but serves as a witness to God's redemptive presence in the world. When we come to the table, we are transformed and become the body of Christ in the world.

Leading from the table is an invitation to the entire congregation to a life of discipleship. Responding to this invitation requires an ongoing and gradual transformation of our lives into the life of Christ. In 2 Corinthians, Paul speaks of this process as part of a continual struggle to allow God to reform his life into a model of Christ's life. For Paul, the language of dying to self is grounded in the imagery of baptism, where the old self is buried and we put on Christ. "So if anyone is in Christ, there is a new creation; everything old has passed away; see, everything has become new!" (5:17). While in some places Paul writes that this transformation is accomplished in baptism, at other times he talks about the ongoing struggle to live according to the spirit rather than the flesh. In Galatians 5, Paul speaks about cultivating the fruits of the Spirit as signs of the new life we have in Christ.

Celebrating communion as an ongoing reaffirmation of our baptism is a primary way of growing into this new life. At the table, we hear and see again Christ's life as a model for our own lives.[8] In response to the invitation to the table, we offer our lives in thanksgiving and service for God's grace. The prayer at the table presents a claim upon our lives that points to ways of Christian life in our world. At the table, we are nourished by the Spirit through the presence of Christ in the elements and in one another. The table provides the deep soil that allows the roots of our Christian life to grow as well as the nourishment that will enable us to blossom and produce fruits of Christian living.

Putting It into Practice

What difference does a communion prayer that speaks of the whole of Christ's life make? Prayers that follow Jesus's life as an outline for Christian discipleship will take distinctive forms within individual communities. Authentic Christian faith is contextual. As the shape of Jesus's life is overlaid upon the contours of our own lives, we find our unique callings. Thus, I am not suggesting a single, prescriptive portrait of the Christian life. Instead, I want to point to unique characteristics of the Jesus narrative within local communities. Below are several vignettes that show the significance of the eucharistic prayer in forming communities that reflect Jesus's commitments and practices.

In downtown Tacoma, Nativity House provided a safe place for homeless people to eat and spend the day while the shelters were closed. Each week members of the staff joined with street people for a brief worship service with communion. A group of homeless people gathered in a small, makeshift chapel. Chronic addiction and mental illness beset many of the participants. Even the act of reading Scripture together took on interesting elements as volunteer readers added their own commentary to the passage. On a Friday morning, I arrived to lead the service. At the time of communion, I offered a brief eucharistic prayer that highlighted Jesus's commitment to serving the poor and alienated. As I began serving the elements of bread and juice to those in the room, I found my own life under conviction for the ways that I often ignored the homeless in my own community. It was clear to me that day that Jesus would have spent much more time in places like this than in many of the places where I did much of my work.

At a worship service on the twentieth anniversary of the assassination of Oscar Romero, Roman Catholic archbishop of El Salvador from 1977 to 1980, a broadly ecumenical group listened to a testimony of Romero's life and teachings. The service included readings from Romero's sermons and teaching about the importance of the church's solidarity with the poor. The communion liturgy was framed by Romero's call to transform our communities of faith into centers for justice: "The church would betray its own love for God and its fidelity to the gospel if it stopped being . . . a defender of the rights of the poor . . . a humanizer of every legitimate struggle to achieve a more just society . . . that prepares the way for the true reign of God in history."[9] Following communion, a group of Native Americans handed out Sacagawea dollar coins to all present as a gift in memory of Romero's sacrifice. For years, I have carried this silver dollar with me as a reminder of the need to share my possessions with those in need.

In a seminary chapel, all present were welcomed to the table to share the bread and the cup. The communion prayer began with a collective retelling of the story of Jesus's life and death. Following this summary, one of the presiders offered an extended prayer that focused on Jesus's solidarity with the poor. He called on the Spirit to enliven us so that we would bear the mark of Christ. As he prayed, he quickly walked down the aisle and pushed open the doors of the chapel. "These doors must be open so that all non-documented people can participate in this meal."[10] Here communion was marked by an awareness of those who were not present and whom we often exclude without acknowledging the way our communities ignore and marginalize them. As we were welcomed to the table to eat and drink, we remembered those who were not present with us around the table.

In recent years, Christians in larger church gatherings have found that communion services can help them negotiate difficult debates. Denominations facing highly contested social issues have discovered that gathering at the table at the start of the meeting improves dialogue and encourages respectful debate. Those who begin a conversation by recognizing Christ's claim on our lives and our unity at the table are more likely to recognize that our theological and doctrinal differences are not enough to cause us to denounce one another.[11] At a presbytery (regional governing body) meeting where an important vote on ordination standards was planned, those planning worship provided an opening communion service that emphasized the unity of the body of Christ. All came forward to receive the elements as a sign of our commitment to follow Christ. The debate that followed the service was heated but respectful. We all discovered that those who break bread together and share the cup find it more difficult to vilify the opponent during debates. Our unity in Christ supersedes our differences of opinion.

Each of these brief descriptions of services presents a way that the outline of Christ's life, death, and resurrection provides a shape to the service and a way to live out these claims on our lives. At stake in these prayers at the table are basic Christian virtues of hospitality, compassion, acceptance, and an openness to the Spirit's transformation of our lives and our community.

Shared Words, Shared Practice

Among friends, gathered around a table,
Jesus took bread,
And, having blessed it,
He broke the bread
And gave it to his disciples, saying,
"This is my body which is given for you."
In the same way he took wine,
And, having given thanks for it,
He poured it out
And gave the cup to his disciples, saying,
"This cup is the new relationship with God,
sealed with my blood.
Take this and share it."[12]

This adaptation of the Words of Institution by the Iona Community points to the importance of sharing a practice of breaking bread and drinking from a cup. It draws from the text of the Words of Institution found in 1 Corinthians 11:23-26 and in Luke 22:19-20. It is important to note that the earliest recorded communion prayers do not include the Words of Institution.[13]

There is great irony that sixteenth-century Reformers who sought to distinguish their communion prayers from the Roman Catholic mass generally adopted the practice of maintaining the Words of Institution as the key element in the prayer at the table. By doing this, they perpetuated earlier decisions that associated the words with the time of the consecration of the elements.[14] By contrast, in the Eastern Church, the emphasis on the role of the Holy Spirit, rather than the use of particular words, was seen as the essential moment in the communion prayer.[15]

Thus, the inclusion of the Words of Institution in the communion prayer affirms a connection between our actions at table and the biblical witness of Jesus's table practice. At the same time, there remains a danger that the Words of Institution are understood as magic words that create a change in the elements or that they are thought to relocate us to the upper room. In our discussion of the thanksgiving prayer at the table, we have stressed the significance of recognizing the many forms of communion meals in the Gospels (both in Jesus's public ministry and in the resurrection accounts). The broader shape of the prayer provides a structure that reinforces a spirit of thankfulness on the part of all who gather around the table. This longer narrative of God's creation and care for all establishes the tone for this gathering. Without this foundation, the use of the Words of Institution reinforces a Maundy Thursday-only approach to communion. A preoccupation with "the night before he died" fails to do justice to the broader witness of Jesus's life, death, and resurrection.

Currently many congregations are committed to stronger and deeper prayer practices around the communion table. These prayers call on the Spirit to transform the bread and wine and the assembly into signs of God's presence in the world. What is at stake here is a significant shift away from the temptation to rely on "magic" words. In most ecumenical table prayers (and in most denominations), the Words of Institution come in the middle of the prayer at table. Often particular gestures are prescribed.[16] One helpful commentary in the *Manual on the Liturgy* by Lutheran scholars Philip Pfatteicher and Carlos Messerli notes that the one presiding at the table is not trying "to imitate what Jesus did at the Last Supper" but seeking to connect Christ's "words of promise visually with *this* bread and *this* cup."[17]

Those of us from the Reformed tradition have a particularly peculiar relationship with the Words of Institution. Historically, this text was used for different purposes at different points in the communion service. At the invitation to the table, the text served as the biblical warrant for celebrating communion. Ron Byars, a Presbyterian liturgical scholar, notes that John Calvin's initial concern was that Scripture be read and proclaimed in association with the gathering at the table.[18] The words were also often used at the end of the prayer in association with the breaking of the bread and the pouring of the wine. Repeating the Words of Institution was another way of heightening their importance. Coupled with words of warning about proper self-examination of one's spiritual state, communion meals often lost any form of joyful celebration.

As a result of an overemphasis on the Words of Institution, the joyful dimension and spirit of gratitude are often minimized or absent. By recovering a full prayer of thanksgiving at the table, we can recover the fuller dimensions of the sacrament. In the context of the full prayer, the Words of Institution find their rightful place alongside the actions of the people who gather around the table. For us as followers of Jesus Christ, these words are part of that which connects us to the witness and action of Jesus of Nazareth.

Making Connections

Last year our seminary community joined in a Good Friday service based on the stations of the cross. The service, though, was not held in a church. Instead, worshipers walked together through neighborhoods and stopped at places where someone had been killed during the previous year. Each stop included a reading from the Gospels that chronicled Jesus's journey to the cross at Golgotha. However, the power of the texts came to life amid the awareness of the violence and senseless deaths in our city. The intersection of the narratives of Scripture with our experiences brings new insight. It is impossible for us to travel back two thousand years to capture a sense of Jesus's death on the cross. However, as we witness the places of violence and death that surround us, stories of injustice in the Gospels take on new life.

Similarly, although gathering around the table for communion even on Maundy Thursday fails to allow us access to the events of the upper room, they begin to come to life as we read and live out of the Scriptures in the midst of our lives. The Words of Institution, like other biblical texts, carry great significance insofar as they ground our lives and actions in the gospel story.

Finally, the presider is not pretending to be Jesus so that the congregation can imagine the way things were done once upon a time. Instead, the one presiding invites us into the gospel story, so that in our association with this text, the Spirit will lead us to discover new ways of life. Here, the biblical language we share and the gestures we use come together to help form us into the pattern of Christ.

Voices of Acclamation

How will we respond to the opportunities and challenges to present Christ to the world? Once we have heard the story of God's persistent love for us and for all the world, and once we have seen the pattern of Christ's life, we are invited to affirm this model for the renewal of our own lives.

In many eucharistic prayers, the primary response is known as the Great Acclamation. The presider expresses deep awe of God's involvement in the redemption of creation, perhaps with words such as: "Great is the mystery of the faith." The people are invited to respond:

> Christ has died.
> Christ is risen.
> Christ will come again.

Through these words worshipers summarize Christ's life in words that are grounded in the incarnation, the resurrection, and the hope of Christ's return. Repetition of this central mystery of the Christian faith is a kind of participation in itself. By expressing this summary, we as worshipers seek to adopt this pattern of self-giving in the belief that God will bring new life to us.

Lasting Reflections

The confirmation class of three teenage boys gathered around my dining-room table. On the table were a communion chalice, a bowl of water, and a Bible. Soon we would add the pizza for dinner. Each week we gathered to study ways that Word and Sacrament shape our lives. On this occasion, we were talking about the role of water in baptism. I asked the boys about how water is used in our lives. There were the usual answers: drinking water, showering, playing in it. Then one young man said that in the Middle Ages, water was used as a mirror. This image of seeing ourselves in the water of baptism has stuck with me through the years. In a similar way, the eucharistic prayer with its portrait of Christ provides an image for our lives. When we come to the table, we look again into the mirror of Christ's life to conform our lives to this image of service, compassion, and self-giving.

In the final analysis, coming to the table is about offering ourselves in thanksgiving for God's grace. As the gospel is faithfully proclaimed and as the assembly acclaims, we are invited to respond in faith. Each time we gather at the table, we grow toward the goal of taking on the pattern of Christ's life in our own lives. Throughout this chapter, the conversations about sacrifice at the table have been reframed to help us realize that God's past actions do not take the place of the call to offer our lives. At the table, through the images of Christ's self-giving, we are invited to present ourselves as a holy offering in service to God's redemptive work in the world.

Hymn for Reflection

Come to the feast of heaven and earth!
Come to the table of plenty!
God will provide for that we need,
here at the table of plenty.

O come and sit at my table
where saints and sinners are friends.
I wait to welcome the lost and lonely
to share the cup of my love.
Come to the feast of heaven and earth!
Come to the table of plenty!
God will provide for that we need,
here at the table of plenty.

O come and eat without money;
come to drink without price.
My feast of gladness will feed your spirit
with faith and fullness of life.
Come to the feast of heaven and earth!
Come to the table of plenty!
God will provide for that we need,
Here at the table of plenty.

My bread will ever sustain you
through days of sorrow and woe.
My wine will flow like a sea of gladness
to flood the depths of your soul.
Come to the feast of heaven and earth!
Come to the table of plenty!
God will provide for that we need,
here at the table of plenty.

Your fields will flower in fullness;
your homes will flourish in peace.
For I, the giver of home and harvest,
will send my rain on the soul.
Come to the feast of heaven and earth!
Come to the table of plenty!
God will provide for that we need,
here at the table of plenty.[19]

Questions for Discussion

1. In the Great Prayer of Thanksgiving, after we hear of God's work in creation and are reminded of our sinfulness and the prophets sent to make our paths straight, the focus turns to Jesus. If you were praying the table prayer, what significant moments in Jesus's life, ministry, death, and resurrection would you lift up? Why?

2. How do you understand the connection between baptism and our calling? How does the language of calling relate to all of Christian life?

3. What is the connection between transforming the bread and wine into the body of Christ and transforming us and the church into Christ's hands and feet and heart in the world and "the assembly into signs of God's presence in the world"?

4. Recite or sing together the Hymn for Reflection on pages 91–92. Why at this "table of plenty" do we offer or tear such small pieces of bread and doll-size cups of wine or juice? What are we saying about our belief that "God will provide for all that we need"?

CHAPTER 7

Experiencing the Spirit and Naming the World before God

Lord, we pray that in your goodness and mercy
your Holy Spirit may descend upon us,
and upon these gifts,
sanctifying them and showing them
to be holy gifts for your holy people . . .[1]

Our group gathered in the college chapel to finish our conference by celebrating Pentecost. The week that we spent together had been a full and busy one with choirs, workshops, seminars, and concerts. We were tired and ready to go home. There in the sanctuary, though, the service took on a life of its own. Scripture came to life through dramatic readings. The sermon recalled the experiences we had shared throughout the week and urged us to live out of these shared experiences. Our gathering around the communion table was framed by the language of baptismal renewal and a call to deepen our lives of faith. Afterward people told me that they did not want to leave. Why is it that when we come together and call upon God's Spirit to bring us new life, we are surprised when it happens? Why are we often content to plod through services the way they have always been done?

The prayer at the communion table frames our world in new ways and invites us to live in light of this new vision. Prayer begins in thanksgiving for God's goodness and faithfulness in creating and sustaining all creation. It continues as we hear the story of Christ's life and are invited to take on this way of life. The next section of the communion prayer focuses on the Spirit's role. Invoking or calling on the Spirit (from the Greek word *epiclesis,* which means "to call upon") leads to a time of intercession that is ultimately led by the Spirit's prompting in our lives. The prayer culminates in our recognition of the opportunity to respond in hope as we live and work for the fulfillment of God's purpose in the world.

Making Space

After tracing the shape of Jesus's life, death, and resurrection, we offer ourselves as disciples to follow in this way, and the prayer at the table makes room for the Spirit's work. Invoking the Spirit is a deliberate act of calling upon God to bring us life.

> Pour out your Holy Spirit on us and on these gifts of bread and wine that the bread we break and the cup we drink may be the communion of the body and blood of Christ.[2]

This act of naming the Spirit as we gather in worship requires special attention. Throughout the Scriptures, the significance of one's name carries spiritual power. In the Hebrew Scriptures, the unspoken name of YHWH is worshiped, but cannot be contained by any single name. Significant leaders throughout the Scriptures receive new names: Abram and Sarai become Abraham and Sarah; Saul of Tarsus becomes Paul. These name changes point to transformational moments in their lives. Even today, the naming of the individual coming for baptism remains a significant moment.

Knowing someone's name allows us to call on them. Hence, invoking the Spirit is an act of naming God and asking for God's presence in our lives as we gather around the table. In this chapter, we will look at distinctive ways in which prayer at the table names and calls upon the Spirit to be present in our lives, in the communion elements that we share, and in the world around us.

Naming and Reclaiming the Spirit's Role

I did not hear much about the Holy Spirit either in the free churches in which I grew up or in the mainline congregations where I
have worshiped for the past twenty-five years. Usually, we left
the talk of the Holy Spirit to the charismatic churches with their
practice of speaking in tongues. The third person of the Trinity
seemed foreign and distant. Occasionally, a Pentecost service or
some other special event gave us a reason to mention the Spirit. By
and large, though, my theology was formed with a restricted role
for the Holy Spirit.

It was only when I went to Scotland on a sabbatical pilgrimage to the Iona Abbey that the Spirit's role became important to
the way that I pray and live. In the wildness of western Scotland,
the ancient Celtic prayers that call upon the Spirit's presence and
protection in the forces of nature shook the timid ways that I had
learned to pray.

> For your Spirit woven into the fabric of creation
> for the eternal overlapping with time
> and the life of earth interlaced with heaven's vitality
> I give you thanks, O God.[3]

On a bitterly cold February day, I sat in the only cafeteria that
was open on the isle of Iona. The wind was howling off the North
Sea. The ferry had been unable to land for the past two days, but
today it was riding the waves to try to reach the docks. Each time
the boat came up to the pier, the wind and waves pushed it past the
landing, and eventually the captain gave up his attempt to land the
boat and turned back toward the island of Mull.

Living and praying on Iona amid the harsh elements of wind
and water and the magnificent beauty of the surroundings challenged the tepid theology of the Spirit with which I had lived. My
growing awareness of God's presence in the gifts of creation and
even in the wildness of creation caused me to reassess my understanding of the Spirit's place in our lives.

That evening on Iona, I walked uphill for evening prayer in the
little chapel behind the abbey. As the winds continued to howl and

rain blew sideways across the island, we listened to the reading for the day: Jesus stilling the storm. The interplay between the Spirit's presence in the wildness (and order) of the world and Christ's presence in the midst of it all pushed me to recognize a need for a more balanced trinitarian theology.

The prayer at the communion table offers a full vision of a vibrant trinitarian theology. It creates space for us to gather in thanksgiving for God's creation and sustained work of redemption and transformation throughout human history. Next, the prayer turns to the story of Jesus as a pattern for our own lives. Finally, the prayer makes room for naming and invoking the Spirit's place and presence. Our act of calling on the Spirit does not magically cause the Spirit to show up (as if it were previously absent). Instead, naming the Spirit is a wake-up call for us to become aware of the Spirit's presence in our lives and in all the stuff of creation. To call upon the Spirit to pour itself out on our lives is to recognize our hunger and thirst for God's presence.

Thich Nhat Hanh, a Buddhist monk, writes about the significance of being mindful in what we do. Eucharist, from his perspective, is about the practice of awareness as we eat one bite of bread and drink one sip of wine. If we can become mindful in this small act, then we will grow in our awareness at other times in our lives. "He [Jesus] knew that if his disciples would eat one piece of bread in mindfulness, they would have real life."[4] For Christians, a growing awareness of the Spirit's work in our lives begins as we get in touch with the mystery of God's presence that is in us and surrounds us. When we call upon the Spirit's presence, the Spirit frames the world, so we can focus on these simple gifts of bread, wine, and one another. In these ordinary things, we learn to discover the Spirit's movement. At the table, we can learn not to take for granted the gift of this bread and the gift of this cup. With this awareness, we discover that all of life is a gift from God.

Interceding

Our awareness of the Spirit's presence in us and around us leads us to call out for the healing of our lives and our world. Our prayers

of intercession expand the process by naming our need and longing for God's wholeness. In intercessory prayer, the presider at the
table opens up space by inviting us to name those places and people in need of God's healing.

Early on a Wednesday morning, we stood quietly in our places
in the sanctuary and listened as the minister called on the Spirit to
be present in us and in the communion elements. Then she called
on us to voice our prayers of thanksgiving and intercession for the
world, the church, and ourselves. The response started as a trickle
as people slowly called out names and places. Then it became a
flood of voices shouting and whispering our prayers together in a
cacophony of sound.

This image of prayer with voices layered one on top of another evokes images of the Pentecost story. In Acts 2, not everyone
understands every word all the time; so too in this experience of
prayer, hearing voices is not the same as understanding each and
every word that is spoken. There is something powerful and mys-
terious about this form of prayer in which together and individu-
ally we speak our requests, not to communicate information for
our neighbors ("Did you know that his aunt is in the hospital?")
but simply to voice our joys and concerns in the context of the
communion prayer that is offered in thanksgiving to God.

As we invoke the Spirit's presence, the Spirit invokes in us a
yearning for the wholeness of our broken lives and world. Trusting in the Spirit's presence, we call out in thanksgiving for the
many blessings of our lives and in supplication for the pain that
is in us and surrounds us. In Romans 8, the apostle Paul offers a
description of the Spirit's work in our lives. Paul begins by urging
us as followers of Jesus Christ to focus on the life of the Spirit. The
Spirit's presence in our lives is grounded in our baptism, where we
receive the sign of Christ in the image of death and resurrection
("we are buried with Christ in baptism and raised to walk in new-
ness of life") and in the sign of the cross marked on our foreheads.
These images point us toward a new way of living in the community of believers. In this new life, Paul points to the Spirit's work
at turning us away from the source of death (trying to fulfill all
the requirements of the law or expending all our energy on satisfy-
ing the flesh). When we obsessively follow ecclesiastical rules or

constantly sate our physical appetites, we leave little room for the Spirit to lead us to new life.

The eucharistic prayer around the table echoes the words of the apostle Paul in the way that it proposes a new orientation for our lives. The Spirit's presence and movement among us prompt us to look at our lives in new ways. As when the waters of baptism covered us and we were named beloved children of God, so too the prayer at the table calls us to move in new directions.

The practice of regularly gathering at the table is in itself a bold attempt to provide a new way of looking at the world. As the prayer at the table begins to permeate our lives, the life of the Spirit that Paul describes becomes a pattern for our lives together. Legalistic ways of doing church, either by doing things the way things have always been done or by conforming to rigid hierarchical power structures, give way to shared ministry. Preoccupation with fulfilling our personal demands yields to caring for our neighbor. This vision of a new community is grounded in Paul's description of life in the Spirit. This Spirit is the one who raises us to resurrection life. As a result, Paul urges us to allow the Spirit to prompt us in our prayers and in our actions. Here, the Spirit pulls us together as the body of Christ to cry out with all of creation for God's redemptive work. In the Spirit, we are made one as we pray and work with hope and patience.[5]

Intercessory prayer around the table includes naming and increasing awareness of the deep needs and brokenness around us. Since in the communion prayer we offer ourselves to God in thanksgiving, the Spirit is at work leading us to intercede not only with our voices but also with our bodies! To pray for the homeless is also to work to provide housing. To pray for those who are hungry compels us to share our food with those in need. To ask God to bring peace in war-torn parts of the world is to commit ourselves to making and keeping peace with those with whom we disagree. Intercessory prayer that is prompted by the Spirit's presence redefines our priorities so that we may faithfully follow in the way of Christ.

Joining the Forces of Nature

Awakening to the Spirit's presence in creation, in our neighbor, and in ourselves is also an opportunity to participate in the redemption of the world around us. The Spirit prompts us to take our place to pray and work for change and transformation. In the words of Philip Newell's prayer:

> Release in me the power of your Spirit
> that my soul may be free
> and my spirit strong.
> Release in me the freedom of your Spirit
> That I may be bridled by nothing but love.[6]

Praying for the Spirit's presence in our lives is one step on the journey toward joining the Spirit's work in our lives and throughout all creation. In this process we are joined with God's Spirit, which ripples through creation and guides us toward the coming of God's reign. Calling upon the Spirit is the starting point for learning to recognize God's presence, pray for one another, and offer our gifts and our lives in service.

A couple years ago, I went with a group from our congregation to Nicaragua. We traveled up into the mountains to visit a small village in the coffee-growing region. We had loaded our suitcases with all the things we could not bear to leave behind. When we arrived at the village, we discovered that the town consisted of a small Pentecostal church, the pastor's home, and a two-room school (first through fourth grades). The only place with a lock was the church, so we were given the keys to the church to store our clothes and belongings. During the week, the congregation gathered each morning and afternoon for Bible study and prayer. The worship services included testimonies and long periods of loud and fervent prayer in which people shouted and hollered in unknown tongues in both praise and lamentation. At times during the prayers, the decibel level was near-deafening as some pleaded with God to bring healing and relief.

In this poverty-stricken village, we found ourselves completely dependent on our hosts. They cooked our meals for us (and often many people gathered around the pastor's house to watch us eat). They guided us through the hills and taught us how to pick the coffee beans from the trees. They opened their homes to us so that we would have places to sleep. They watched out for us and shared with us the difficulties and struggles of their daily lives. On our last morning in the village, the congregation gathered in the church to offer us one final gift. During the prayer time, they called upon the Spirit to take us down safely from the mountain and to protect us on our way home. They had already given us everything else they had to offer, and this prayer of intercession was the final blessing that they bestowed on us.

Praying for the Spirit's presence is a starting place on the journey toward a life of generosity. As the communion prayer prompts us to take the signs of Christ's life on our lives, so too the Spirit breaks through the tight grasp we hold on our lives and our belongings. Our language of personal possession runs contrary to the movement of the prayer at table that begins by recognizing that all of life is a part of God's good gift of creation, that presents the claim of Christ on our lives, and that calls upon the Spirit to prompt us so that we will live out these deep truths. As we grow into this prayer, we learn to recognize that all of our belongings, our health, and our other blessings are gifts from God for us to share with those around us. As we have seen previously in chapter 1, in Acts the first followers of Jesus shared all their possessions with any who had need. They lived together with a deep awareness of their solidarity and dependence on God.

Worship leaders who demonstrate an openness to the demands of the communion prayer give testimony in the words of the table prayer to ways that the Spirit is prompting us to change our lives. Communities that live out these virtues with glad and generous hearts welcome strangers and those in need to gather around the communion table and to break bread with us at other tables through the week. Some congregations have discovered that placing the bread from the communion table on the potluck table for the congregational gathering in fellowship hall is a way to point to the close ties between the tables where we eat. When all are welcomed to the communion table, then it becomes clear that we need to display similar hospitality at our dining-room tables.

A student in one of my classes reported that when a homeless person showed up at her church, she decided to take him out to eat. They walked down the street to a local diner and shared a meal. The individual was deeply grateful, but more important, the student found herself thinking differently about time and meals. It is easy to become so busy with our routines that we pass by the people who live alongside us. Taking time to respond to the needs of those around us helps us rediscover our connection with one another. Eating together builds relationships that transcend barriers created by society and class structures.

As the Spirit makes room for new life and relationships in our lives, we discover opportunities that surround us each day to respond to those who are in need. A good friend of mine who lives in New York tells a story about sitting on the steps of a nearby church waiting for someone to open the doors so he could go in and rehearse his music for an upcoming worship service. He was surrounded by homeless people who had spent the night on the steps of the church. As he sat there with them, they began to sing and pray together. One older man sat on the steps and sang old hymns with him. Now each time he runs into the older gentlemen he met that day, he digs through his pockets to find a little money to share with him. The Spirit's presence in the face of his neighbor, whom he learned to recognize on the steps of the church, has prompted him to respond in new ways.

This openness to God's presence within us and surrounding us begins as we allow the communion prayer to shape our vocabulary in order that we experience the world anew. Calling on the Spirit at the table is more than a formality by the presider. Together we learn to call out to the Spirit so that our lives will become full and open to God's work in the world.

Send Us Out

The church assembles not only to gather around the table and to allow the prayer to shape our lives. We also come together so that we may go out from our assemblies and live in the light of this new vision. "Send us out to be the body of Christ in the world."[7] This dramatic reversal in language and imagery breaks open the normal way we hear the prayer at the table. Suddenly, the actions at the table are not simply about breaking this loaf of bread and pouring out this cup. Through the Spirit, these dramatic actions present the body of Christ to us. However, communion does not end at this point. Instead, we become communion vessels as well. We are the ones who leave the table to live as the body of Christ *in the world*. This bold claim relocates our notions of where the body of Christ resides. Far beyond the safe walls of the sanctuaries, we go out as incarnational signs of Christ's presence in our lives.

When we take this language seriously, then our experience of the sacraments is greatly expanded. Communion cannot be restricted to the ten to fifteen minutes when we gather inside the church. Instead this prayer and these acts become foundational for the rest of our lives. Through the Spirit's power, we go out as Christ's body in the world to provide sustenance for those who hunger and thirst for the bread that comes down from heaven (John 6:58) and for the living water that quenches our thirst (John 4:14). In the words of the communion prayer, we become sacramental signs as we point to God's grace, which surrounds us and sustains us.

Once again, the words of the communion prayer draw deeply from Pauline theology. In 1 Corinthians 12, Paul speaks of the way the Spirit provides gifts for the community to live together. These gifts are for the edification or building up of the common good. Paul speaks of the one body of Christ that we become as we live in community. Through the Spirit's work that is grounded in our baptism, we are the body of Christ (1 Cor. 12:27).

Formulas and Conclusions

How do you end a prayer? Like other prayers, communion prayers have a certain form. As we have seen, the prayer at the table takes a trinitarian shape in the way that the sections of the prayer speak of God as creator of the world, of Christ who models for us a life of faithfulness, and of Spirit who prompts us to live as the body of Christ in the world. Thus, while the prayer is implicitly shaped by its trinitarian framework, the close of the prayer takes on explicit trinitarian language. This prayer of thanksgiving is offered in the name of the one God known to us in the baptismal formula of Father, Son, and Holy Spirit. An often overlooked significance of this trinitarian benediction to the communion prayer is that it provides a way for us to renew our baptismal vows as we respond to the presence of God as Father, Son, and Holy Spirit.

Some recent eucharistic prayers have provided alternative ways to retain trinitarian references while providing images that are biblically grounded and inclusive. For example, Gail Ramshaw has written a prayer that concludes with the following words:

> You, Holy God, Holy One, Holy Three,
> Our Life, our Mercy, our Might,
> Our Table, our Food, our Server,
> Our Rainbow, our Ark, our Dove,
> Our Sovereign, our Water, our Wine,
> Our Light, our Treasure, our Tree,
> Our Way, our Truth, our Life.[8]

The beauty of this prayer is that it expands the way that we see God in Scripture. Expanding our trinitarian vocabulary provides ways for us to recognize the dynamic presence of God in the world around us.

Giving a Great Amen

My predecessor at the seminary taught our community the importance of voicing our assent to the communion prayer. Whenever he presided at the table, his prayer followed the trinitarian formula, and then he paused and waited for the congregation to respond.[9] This response at the close of the communion prayer is known as the Great Amen, and it is where we raise our voices to concur with the prayer. There is evidence that in the early centuries of the church's life, the communion prayer was itself a statement of faith for the community. Thus as we voice our assent to the prayer at the table, we reaffirm our faith in the God known to us as three-in-one.

As we have already seen, our response is not simply a verbal expression, but a form of assent by which we offer our lives in gratitude to God. Prayer at table provides ongoing catechetical opportunities for our faith to grow deeper and more whole as we take in these words and live them out daily. Our verbal agreement with the prayer offered at the table leads us to receive these gifts of bread and wine and to carry the blessings of these gifts beyond the doors of our churches and into our communities. In congregations where individuals walk in procession to the table to receive the elements, the act of getting up and coming forward is an additional sign of commitment. As we have seen in this section, the Spirit upon whom we call is the One who prompts us in our actions to receive and live as the body of Christ.

Hymn for Reflection

Spirit blowing through creation,
Spirit burning in the skies,
Let the hope of your salvation fill our eyes:
God of splendor, God of glory,
You who light the stars above,
All the heavens tell the story of your love.

As you moved upon the waters,
As you ride upon the wind,
Move us all, your sons and daughters deep within;
As you shaped the hills and mountains,
Formed the land and filled the deep,
Let your hand renew and waken all who sleep.

Spirit renewing the earth,
Renewing the hearts of all people:
Burn in the weary souls,
Blow through the silent lips,
Come now awake us,
Spirit of God.

Love that sends the rivers dancing,
Love that waters all that lives,
Love that heals and holds and rouses and forgives;
You are food for all your creatures,
You are hunger in the soul,
In your hands the brokenhearted are made whole.

All the creatures you have fashioned,
All that live and breathe in you,
Find their hope in your compassion, strong and true;
You, O Spirit of salvation,
You alone, beneath, above,
Come, renew your whole creation in your love.

Spirit renewing the earth,
Renewing the hearts of all people:
Burn in the weary souls,
Blow through the silent lips,
Come now awake us,
Spirit of God.[10]

Questions for Discussion

1. Consider the worship experience in the college chapel. How much is a one-hour service ingrained in the life of your congregation? What is the relationship between a limited time for worship and the freedom of the Spirit in various forms, such as extended prayer, a long but good sermon, or the spontaneous repetition of a hymn refrain?

2. Rather than setting aside a time of praying for others, what do you think of embedding those requests in the communion prayer? Do you think it is necessary after speaking a person's name to say that he or she is being prayed for—or, given that God knows our needs before we speak them (Matt. 6:8), is it enough to hear the name aloud? Or in the case of the "loud prayer" (as Korean Presbyterians call it) described, is simply saying a prayer aloud sufficient, whether or not anyone else clearly hears it?

3. In Romans 8 Paul writes that "creation groans with sighs too deep for words." How have you experienced silence in the Lord's Supper? How might silence help or hinder this or other parts of a worship service?

4. Meals are often associated with "hearth and home," security and comfort. Yet at the Lord's Table we are sent out into the world. What is the relationship between being fed and being sent out?

5. Recite or sing together the Hymn for Reflection on pages 104–105. What does it mean to you that the Spirit that first blew over creation now breathes in you? And that it breathes not just in you, but through all of God's church and out into all of God's world? What is the relationship between the Wind blowing over the waters creating the earth and blowing over the waters in which you were baptized?

CHAPTER 8

Eating with Our Eyes Open

Give us today our daily bread.
Forgive us our sins
As we forgive those who sin against us.[1]

Following the Great Amen, when the congregation voices its assent to the communion prayer, the assembly joins together in the Lord's Prayer. With one voice, we pray as Jesus taught us. There is no evidence that the Lord's Prayer was part of the eucharistic prayer in the earliest centuries of Christian faith. Nevertheless, the prayer has become a significant and historic ecumenical witness of unity among Christians.[2] The Lord's Prayer reinforces a central Reformation principal that the prayer at table belongs to the assembly and not simply to the presider. As we recite the Lord's Prayer, our voice is joined with all who gather around the table.

While some feminists have raised important concerns about the exclusive masculine language of the Lord's Prayer, some balance can be provided in the liturgy by making sure that the imagery of the eucharistic prayer includes both feminine and masculine imagery. Previous chapters have provided suggestions that broaden the vocabulary in many eucharistic prayers. One important reason to use the language of "Our Father" is to reinforce baptismal language. Here the prayer connects to the claims of the baptismal liturgy that we are baptized in the name of the Father, Son, and Holy Spirit. In baptism, we are identified as beloved children (sons and daughters) of God. The language provides a clear parallel to the narrative of divine blessing in Jesus's baptism ("This is my Son, the Beloved, with whom I am well pleased" [Matt. 3:17]). The Lord's

Prayer places us in solidarity with our brother Jesus, who has gone before us and teaches us to pray. Finally, the prayer summarizes our commitment to follow in the way of Christ.

Give Us This Day

Many good references and commentaries explore meanings of each phrase in the Lord's Prayer. In the context of prayer at the communion table, it is important to note the associations between the language of the Lord's Prayer and the actions of the assembly as it gathers around the table. One example of these associations is found in the phrase "Give us this day our daily bread." As part of the communion prayer, the images of "day" and "bread" both take on new meanings. This day that is given to us is celebrated by Christians as the Lord's Day. Throughout the history of the church, Christians have gathered on the first day of the week as a way to commemorate Christ's resurrection. In the early church, this first day of the week was also thought of as the eighth day, a day of new creation in which God brings new life. In this sense, the day when we gather to worship assumes the role of both the beginning and end of creation. Once again, baptismal imagery lies beneath the surface. As church buildings were built and baptismal space established, these notions of the eight days of creation and new creation influenced the baptismal space, which in many places was built in the shape of an octagon to point to the new understanding of time symbolized in baptism. Thus, the one who passes through these waters enters into a new day with a new understanding of time. This perspective grows out of Christ's resurrection on the first day of the week and looks to the eighth day as the culmination of time.

When we pray the words "Give us this day," we acknowledge that the Lord's Day (like each day) comes as a gift from God. To gather each Lord's Day is to establish a rhythm for our lives that shapes an understanding of all time as gifts from God. In this perspective, the artificial separation of sacred and secular yields to an awareness that each moment is sacred.

In a similar way, the prayer of thanksgiving for "our daily bread" points to all bread (and wine) as a gift from God to be eaten in gratitude for the bountiful sustenance of creation. Here, the church's voice must more clearly reject claims that this bread and wine are somehow supernatural elements. As bread and wine (ordinary things), they are already signs of God's presence and blessing among us. On this point, Calvin and the Reformers are once again helpful. The sacrament of Holy Communion is not created by the priest, particular words, or the transformation of the elements themselves. Instead, the Spirit's presence in the assembly as it gathers around the table enables us to recognize God's presence in the gifts of bread and wine. Perhaps another way to look at communion is that our awareness of God's provision in this bread that is blessed and broken at the Lord's Table leads us to grow in awareness that each day's bread is blessed. The Lord's Table challenges our notions of self-reliance, that we can work hard enough to provide for ourselves what we need. Slowly, as we gather regularly around the Lord's Table, the prayer of thanksgiving and the Lord's Prayer open us up to an understanding of our deep dependence on God's grace and sustenance for each day and for each meal. The testimony of the early followers of Jesus in Acts 2 is that breaking bread together created in them glad and generous hearts. Coming to the table regularly is a way of cultivating our hearts so that we will live in thanksgiving and share with those who are in need.

With Open Eyes

The Emmaus road narrative in the Gospel of Luke witnesses to this understanding of the divine presence in the ordinary moments of life. Luke recounts the story of two weary travelers trudging home after the events of the Passover in Jerusalem. Their hopes for a Messiah were dashed as they witnessed the arrest and crucifixion of Jesus of Nazareth. They are joined on their journey by a stranger. Their journey down the road to Emmaus becomes a time of catechesis. They retell the experiences they have shared together in

Jerusalem during the past few days. The stranger, who assumes the role of teacher, reframes these experiences by placing them in the context of Scripture. Their understanding of their experiences and feelings is shaped by hearing Moses and the prophets interpreted. Thus, congregations gather to hear Scripture read and proclaimed as preparation for coming to the table. As it was for the disciples on the Emmaus road, Scripture serves us as a primary resource that leads us to the table. The word whets our appetite.

While explanation is one part of the stranger's teaching, the result is not rational insight (the "aha!" moment comes later in the narrative). Instead, Cleopas and the other yearn for more. They urge Jesus to stay with them, and they invite him to the table to eat with them. In the language of our prayers at table, we generally depict Christ as host. When we pay close attention to the role of host within the Gospels, we gain additional insight into those who serve at the table. In the Gospel meals, others often serve as host. Those who gather around the table encounter Christ. Liturgical language often depicts Christ as host in some instances to undergird the church's power and authority.[3] At the same time, the presider assumes Christ's place as host and thereby enforces our rules about who can preside. Careful attention to passages like the Emmaus road text may provide other models of leadership at the table that will challenge current practices.[4] As a starting place, the Emmaus text provides a model for reclaiming our role as hosts at table that is rooted in our desire to encounter the presence of the risen Christ. Here, the opportunity to serve as host is linked to our hunger rather than to our abilities or accomplishments.

Breaking of the Bread

In the Emmaus road narrative, the critical moment arrives when the two disciples are at the table and Jesus breaks the bread. Then, their eyes are opened and they recognize him. This text underscores the importance of the actual practice of breaking the bread as we celebrate communion. I remember visiting a stunning church on one occasion. I watched as a beautiful loaf of bread was carried down the aisle before the prayer of thanksgiving, only to be shocked that the presider broke the bread in a way that none of us could actually witness it.

By contrast, St. James Church, Piccadilly, in London, has adopted the practice of breaking the bread (or in this case, a large wafer) multiple times as the presider turns to face in each direction. This fourfold practice follows a simple form that allows for variations. The basic pattern is:

To the East: in honor of all those who love God
To the South: for the earth
To the West: for the broken and disposed
To the North: for the brokenness within us.[5]

A variation on these words emphasizes the solidarity of people from different religious faiths who seek God. It includes the recognition of the goodness of the earth that provides us with food and invites us to care for the earth. It challenges us to recognize and provide for those who are poor, who do not have enough to eat. It makes room for those who are poor to join us at our tables. In this process, we recognize our own dependence and need for God and for one another.

This dramatic practice of breaking the bread brings to life the image of eyes wide open from Luke's Gospel. As our eyes are opened to the presence of the risen Christ in the breaking of the bread, our eyes become open to the goodness and brokenness in the world, in our neighbors, and in ourselves. This practice of breaking bread is grounded in a conviction that the celebration of communion is not simply for a local congregation. Donald Reeves, former rector of St. James Church, Piccadilly, reflects: "It makes a public statement about the renewal and healing of the planet. And the breaking is the place where this is made explicit."[6]

Similarly, in some traditions the presider pours wine from the pitcher (or flagon) to the chalice to portray dramatically that the cup of the new covenant is poured out for us. In other traditions, the presider lifts up the cup as a sign that we offer this cup in thanksgiving to God. These gestures draw the congregation into embodying the table prayer in our lives. When we break bread and drink wine at our household tables, we carry with us bodily memories and associations from our experiences at church. At celebrative meals, we raise a toast to honored guests and special occasions. I am not suggesting that we adopt the practice of toasting at communion (although the current use of individual plastic cups is a watered-down version of this practice). I am suggesting that presiders pay close attention to the gestures and physical actions at the table. If eating and drinking are elements central to the Lord's Supper, then leaders should find ways to highlight the acts. When sitting in the congregation, I have often noticed that those who distribute the elements are frequently served without regard to those in the pews. Congregational members can often see only the backs of those who stand around the table. Careful analysis of our actions around the table will help us identify ways to improve our presiding, so that we maintain focus on the central elements of bread and wine.[7]

Picturing the Table

An ancient mural in a catacomb in Rome portrays the significance of breaking bread in the life of the ancient church. The mural, which dates from the late second century, is painted on an arch opposite the entrance to the chapel. The portrait shows a group gathered at table and includes a woman seated in the midst of five men and an older bearded man at the end of the table. The older man, seated in the place of honor, extends his arms over the table and is in the act of breaking the bread to share in the meal. On the table in front of him is also a large chalice, as well as a plate with two fish and five other pieces of bread. At the ends of the table are seven baskets to hold additional bread.[8]

The mural provides significant evidence that the eucharistic meal played a formative role in the Christian community in Rome. First, it reinforces notions of table fellowship that we have explored throughout this book. Here, in the catacombs, the portrait of life above the burial spaces is centered on the practice of breaking bread, sharing wine, and eating together. Men and women sit together and share alike in this meal. Second, the mural clearly portrays a biblical reference to the feeding of the five thousand. The two fish and five loaves of bread as well as the seven baskets all recall the Gospel portrait. Several aspects of the image are worth noting:

- This community selected a meal practice from Jesus's life and ministry as the primary lens for Eucharist. Many of us come from communities where the Last Supper (and particularly Leonardo da Vinci's portrait) has become the sole source of imagery. Adding other images will help us reexamine our practices, so that we can develop a broader vision and a more faithful repertoire of Gospel and early Christian meal practices.

- Perhaps a central reason for the mural depicting the feeding of the five thousand relates to the story's central thrust that Jesus's ministry includes the Gentile community. Matthew, Mark, and Luke all press the point that the gathering of the leftover bread is to provide food for the Gentiles. The miracle of the feeding of the five thousand is extended beyond the gathering so that others may share in the event. Both Matthew and Mark link the feeding of the five thousand with a second miracle story of the feeding of the four thousand. Between these two narratives, Jesus and his disciples cross over the Sea of Galilee into Gentile territory.

- The seven baskets surrounding the table provide a sense of wholeness or completeness as well as a sense of the abundance of food that is shared. Here the portrait challenges the ways that many of us celebrate communion with meager cubes of bread and sips of juice. This mural draws on the dramatic notions that God provides an overabundance of food so that all will have enough to eat.[9]

- Given its location in the burial site, the mural sets this scene of shared life alongside the reality of death. Even surrounded by death, the mural reinforces the importance of the regular gathering and celebration around the table. It offers a vision of hope for the time when all will gather around the table in the kingdom of God. Perhaps even the use of seven people in the mural is a way of foreshadowing a hope of completion (the number seven often signifies perfection or completion) that all will gather around the table in the days when God's reign will be manifest to all.

What is crucial is that leaders find ways to broaden the language, images, and portrayals of communion. When the Lord's Supper is shrunk to pictures, sermons, and language that build solely on an imagined portrait of the upper room on Maundy Thursday, then it is little wonder that our celebrations of communion are often tepid. Only by recovering the richness of biblical allusions, early Christian imagery, and the diversity of Christian practice will we be able to reclaim the table's central role in our worship and the close connection with other tables around which we gather to eat and drink.

The Vanishing Sight

The table as place of encounter is not a final stopping point. Instead, the events at table prepare us for further engagement in the world. In our reading of the Emmaus text, we discover that the experience of Christ's presence is fleeting and energizing. In the moment of recognition, the stranger vanishes, as if he cannot be contained by word, event, or encounter. At the same time, the experience transforms the disciples from tired and discouraged to full of energy and desire as they rush to share the encounter with their friends back in Jerusalem.

I recently participated in a weeklong worship conference on celebrating the fifty days of the Easter season. Each day we gathered for worship that included a reaffirmation of our baptism and communion. The schedule was full. The weather was hot. The classes and service wore me down as the week went on. On the last evening, we celebrated a Pentecost service full of song, life, and movement. Although we were tired, we were also energized by the experience. Participants declared that they wished the service had just kept on going! Scripture read and proclaimed, bread broken and shared revived our bodies and spirits and energized us for sharing and service.

Effective leaders plan and lead worship that energizes the assembly. Taking time carefully and thoughtfully to craft a service increases worshipers' ability to experience God's presence. However, it is not our planning and effort that bring renewal. Ultimately, we are dependent upon the Spirit's presence to bring life to those who gather around the table. Part of the mystery of the sacraments resides in the way that we cannot confine or determine the outcome. This transitory element invites humility on the part of leaders whose openness, presence, and hospitality provide space so that the eyes of those who gather at table may be opened.

Eat This Bread, Drink This Wine

A powerful aroma wafted out of the little bakery down the street from my home. I nearly always went into the shop as I carried my laptop computer to the coffee shop further down the street. The smell of the bread, the beauty of the crust, the flavor and texture of the rolls were an invitation to take and eat.

Similarly, one of my students recently described a visit he and his wife made to a local vineyard. They discovered that the vintner produced the wine for the local Episcopal church. When they asked him about the process, he answered: "These are grapes to everyone but me. I know what is in them before anyone else does. I can taste things that are not there yet but could be there with the right care. And I pick the ones that are used [in the service]. I do not take this lightly. God gave me the gift of winemaking. I do all of this in service to God."[10] Participation in the congregation's worship transformed this person's own livelihood and expanded his understanding of service. His vocation, his own calling, became grounded in the act of gathering at the table.

The gifts of bread and wine on the table are important in their own right. While the efficacy of the communion is certainly not dependent on the quality of the elements, these things themselves serve as momentary containers for the presence of the holy. Our associations (especially kinetic memories of eating and drinking) are grounded in our sensory responses to this bread that we eat and this wine that we drink. Thus, the choices that we make in regard to the elements that are served shape our experience at the table.

Three of us who had gone on a three-day spiritual retreat in New Harmony, Indiana, drove back to Louisville. Our time together had been enriching, enlightening, and profound. So as we headed home, we pondered how to mark this occasion. We opted for a final meal together. In a wonderful restaurant in Louisville, we shared good wine, relished crab cakes, and ended with crème brûlée. The three of us now live in different cities, but when we see each other we recall our experiences on retreat together. Our remembering always includes the meals we ate, the particular tastes that we shared, and the joy that seized us around the table.

Recently, I took pictures of the tables where I ate each day. Over a two-week period, I created a photographic journal of the places as well as the food I ate at breakfast, lunch, and dinner. Often breakfast was a cup of tea and slice of toast on the coffee table in my living room. Other meals included elaborate buffets with a variety of options. The process helped me think about the places where I eat, what I eat, and the people with whom I eat. What I also noticed was that during this two-week period, I was never in a church where communion was served. Alongside the pictures of plentiful meals, I added pictures of empty communion tables—of patens and chalices without elements.

Connecting the communion table with the other tables where we eat requires thoughtful attention. The practice of weekly communion provides a basic starting place by serving as a norm for table practices. Using natural, whole-grain bread and good table wine as elements on the table undergirds the experience of encountering Christ in the gifts that come from this good earth. Highly processed elements, fancy or pretentious offerings, or attempts to appeal to pop culture (Coca-Cola and french fries) miss the point. The gospel shapes the gatherings at table around ordinary meals that become revelatory but defy containment.

Giving Thanks—Before and After

Throughout this extended discussion of the Great Prayer of Thanksgiving, we have drawn attention to the importance of acknowledging our gratitude for God's commitment to creating, calling, redeeming, and sustaining us and the creation. This posture of thanksgiving provides a foundation for our response—which is to maintain a sense of gratitude throughout our life. When we receive the bread and wine, we affirm these gifts with an amen. When communion servers offer worshipers the "bread of life" and the "cup of salvation," they connect the gift of this bread and this cup to all of God's good gifts to us this day.

As mentioned earlier, the acts of eating and drinking are themselves important, and in recent decades some traditions have recognized that significance. Medieval practices marginalized the congregation to the point that the laity were required to receive the elements only once a year, and for centuries, Roman Catholic laypeople were permitted to receive only the bread. Minimizing the elements (and Protestants have done this with the use of tiny shot glasses) reinforces the tendency to turn the Eucharist into a spiritual, otherworldly exercise. By its very nature as a physical act, the meal demands that we pay close attention to our bodies. In this sense, partaking of communion is an incarnational event. Our bodily participation, taking in the elements as God's sign and gift to us, gives witness to a belief that in this act, God is present with *and* in us.

Even the method of distributing the elements carries theological implications. Coming forward to the table to receive the elements is an active response to the gospel. It involves participation as a community, which moves forward together, and as individuals, who receive the elements from the servers. Congregations that have a history of passing the elements through the pews claim an understanding of the importance of serving one another. Smaller congregations may have the advantage of adopting practices that build on the strengths of different patterns. For example, one new-church development meets in the cafeteria of a local school. Each Sunday the congregation places a lunch table at the front of the room. The table is flanked by a small lectern holding the Bible from which the lessons are read and a pedestal with a large bowl of water for baptism. At the time of the prayer of thanksgiving, the pastor invites the congregation to gather around the table. The pastor offers a simple yet rich prayer. The bread and wine are passed around the circle from member to member. Here the act of re-membering shows relational qualities of service. Once all are served, the community joins hands and prays together.

Prayer after communion extends our thanksgiving for God's goodness. In the prayer, we give thanks for the opportunity to participate in this event again. By connecting to the extended prayer before the meal, this prayer shows the importance of practicing gratitude at all times. It also challenges the perfunctoriness with which we sometimes pray before a meal. Instead, we learn how to pray without ceasing, to surround all our activities with prayer.

Go in Peace

The word *mass* is derived from the Latin expression at the conclusion of the Eucharist: *Ita missa est*. "Go, it is sent." The directness of the expression connects our worship with our service in the world. This meal does not pull us out of the world. It sends us into the world. It is sent, or—to follow up on the theme from the Emmaus narrative—this moment has vanished. It is time to move on. Like the food the disciples shared in Emmaus, the meal prepares us to reengage in our work (as carried out in our vocations).

To go in peace is to carry the spirit of Christ with us as we leave church. Scripture also urges that we gather for worship in the spirit of peace. Jesus tells his followers that we are to seek reconciliation with our brothers or sisters in preparation for worship (Matt. 5:23-24). The early Christian practice of sharing a holy kiss as a sign of peace underscores the importance of reconciliation, which begins within the Christian community and extends into the world.

Recovering practices that show our hunger for God, our openness to one another, and our connection to the world around us is a central ingredient in the renewal of the church's worship. Leaders who model these traits demonstrate basic Christian practices, preparing the way for churches to move towards wholeness. The table as place of welcome and hospitality can help lead to the healing of the rifts and divisions that often separate us. At the same time, leaders who point out ways to connect these practices in church with practices in the world challenge the notion of communion as a private act that Christians do behind closed doors.

Hymn for Reflection

The time was early evening,
the place a room upstairs;
The guests were the disciples,
few in number and few in prayers.
Oh, the food comes from the baker;
the drink comes from the vine;
The words come from the Savior,
"I will meet you in bread and wine."

The company of Jesus
had met to share a meal;
The One who made them welcome
had much more to reveal.
Oh, the food comes from the baker;
the drink comes from the vine;
The words come from the Savior,
"I will meet you in bread and wine."

"The bread and body broken,
the wine and blood outpoured,
The cross and kitchen table
are one by my sign and word."
Oh, the food comes from the baker;
the drink comes from the vine;
The words come from the Savior,
"I will meet you in bread and wine."

Christ Jesus, now among us,
confirm our faith's intent,
As, with your words and actions,
we unite in this sacrament.
Oh, the food comes from the baker;
the drink comes from the vine;
The words come from the Savior,
"I will meet you in bread and wine."[11]

Questions for Discussion

1. What is the relationship between the bread and the Lord's Table, and the request in the Lord's Prayer to "give us this day our daily bread"?

2. Think about the bread that makes the feast of the Lord's Supper.

- How does it smell, taste, and feel?
- Is it homemade by a church member or store-bought?
- Do the size and texture point to the abundance of Living Bread?
- Is there a "demonstration loaf" that is broken and other bread that is shared? What does this practice suggest?
- Does the loaf have a cut in it to ease tearing, or is the whole loaf torn? What does this practice symbolize?
- Are precut cubes of bread or wafers served, or are pieces or chunks torn from the loaf? What is being communicated by each of these practices?

3. Where have you celebrated the Lord's Supper besides a church sanctuary on a Sunday morning? Outdoor worship? Seated around a table in the fellowship hall? At a wedding or a funeral? At other places or times? What has been the experience or significance of these services?

4. Recite or sing together the Hymn for Reflection on page 119. Much of the Lord's Supper centers on what we receive. But in the hymn, the baker brings bread and Jesus brings the words. What do you bring to the table? As your closing prayer, go around the room naming a gift that you bring to the feast.

CHAPTER 9

Eucharist as a Way of Life

Take. Bless.
Break. Give.

A small group of hikers gathered at the base of the mountain. They were heading up into the woods. A couple of the climbers had some experience, while others who were new to climbing stretched nervously. For the first couple of hours, they marched with ease up the narrow trail. After a while, though, the path began to be covered by dense overgrowth. Their pace slowed. By mid-afternoon, they were walking in circles lost in the forests high in the hills. In a small clearing, they paused and considered their options. They pooled the assets in their backpacks: six energy bars, two bags of granola, and several bottles of water. Slowly, the leader took two of the energy bars, made the sign of the cross on her body, and broke the bars into pieces. A helicopter suddenly appeared overhead and the group waved wildly to the pilot. As the chopper descended to a nearby clearing, they ate with a new joy.

A Pattern for Living

The four basic gestures of taking, blessing, breaking, and giving that are at the center of the eucharistic prayer provide a shape or outline for Christian life. As we have considered the pattern of prayer at Table, these gestures have provided a basis for Christian action at the Lord's Table and at the other tables around which we gather. We have explored ways in which the shape of the prayer at table builds on the shape of the gospel as it provides a pattern for our lives.

In a world driven by consumption and greed, the notion of *taking* can be easily misconstrued as an excuse to grab what one wants. In a time when there is an ever-growing gap between the haves and the have-nots, taking is not a justification for personal gain at another's expense, either for those who hoard assets or for those who seek a violent overthrow of the current economic system. Instead, taking is rooted in the language of the prayer at table. In this context, taking is more akin to the act of receiving. For example, in the Gospel scenes of the feeding of the multitudes, the act of Jesus's taking bread is rooted in an act of generosity—in one instance shared by a young boy who offers his lunch and, by the presence of God, provides enough for all to eat. Jesus accepts what is offered. Similarly, at the table we practice receiving in gratitude that which is handed to us as a sign of God's faithfulness.

Blessing is the peculiar act of naming God's presence in our actions. To invoke God's name in our daily lives is to recognize the presence that is already there. In this act of naming, we look for the sacred characteristics that run through our lives. All times have the potential to reveal the divine presence as we name and discover God's presence. As we take bread, we give thanks for it so that we are open to encountering God as we gather around the table. At other times in our lives, we look back like Jacob and declare, "Surely God was in this place." The act of blessing, as the opposite of cursing, recognizes God's presence and favor on those who have gathered.

Breaking is the most problematic of these practices. In one sense, breaking is simply the act of dividing what we have to share with those around us. It is rooted in the vision of the early Christian community in Acts 2, which shared all things in common and distributed as any had need. In another sense, breaking the bread metaphorically acknowledges the brokenness of our lives and our need to seek God's healing. This form of brokenness is rooted in the Gospel narrative of Christ's brokenness on the cross. Christ's act of faithful witness over against the power structures of the day leads to God's work of resurrection.

Giving begins with the simple acts of sharing that are noted above, but in following the pattern of Christ, it moves to the point of self-giving. As the communion prayer offers the gospel proclamation, it claims us as participants in this narrative. As we respond fully to the invitation to the table, we find our lives reshaped in the pattern of Jesus Christ.

These central gestures of the Christian life are offered in memory and hope. In memory of Christ's faithful witness of taking, blessing, breaking, and giving, we participate in this pattern. We offer our lives in hope that the One who was present in Christ's ministry will be present in our service. We anticipate God's multiplying the gifts that we bring in order for God's reign of peace and justice to take hold. In the face of death, we cling to the promise and power of the resurrection.

This is the eucharistic life. It is receiving and accepting the mark of Christ's life upon our own lives. It is trusting the Spirit to call us away from the selfish patterns of greed, consumption, self-absorption, and deceit. Celebrating communion regularly in a community that fully participates in the prayer at table allows the narrative of thanksgiving to take root and grow in our lives. Congregations that steadfastly hold and embody the prayer and action around the table discover reliable resources for growth and maturity in the Christian faith.

The Purpose of the Assembly

Let's be clear about our aim as we seek to recover a fuller service of Word and Table. It is not enough simply to claim that the church should gather weekly to read Scripture and celebrate communion. Neither Jesus nor Scripture mandates a particular pattern for the gathering of believers. Throughout church history other patterns have developed, and simply to refer to them as deviant seems polemical. As congregations seek direction for renewal, questions of authority rise to the surface. Who will determine the basic patterns for the gathered assembly and on what grounds will these decisions be made? All proposals for the community's gathering carry assumptions about the role of authority for leaders who establish and maintain certain practices and priorities in a congregation's eucharistic celebrations.

Ronald Grimes, a leading scholar in ritual studies, suggests five perspectives about how authority in liturgical or ritual practice is established and maintained.

1. *Through endorsement.* There are a variety of forms that this perspective might take, but in general it points to an individual or group that establishes the pattern as normative. When it comes to communion practices, many have claimed a divine directive for the sacraments.[1] While the evidence that God instructed the church to celebrate communion is difficult to discern, the importance here is that God serves as the authority for our practice (and equally important, any objection to current practice is an objection against God's commands!).

2. *Through tradition.* While there may have been a divine initiative, this perspective maintains that the authoritative tradition provides a sense of continuity by asserting that present practices continue the way things have always been done.

3. *By following the rules.* From this perspective, the current practice has been received from and prescribed by past leaders and codified in its present form. The role of leaders and participants is to follow the guidelines that have been handed on to them. This perspective is particularly common in traditions where liturgical and sacred books prescribe ways of gathering.

4. *Through the assembly's commitment and work to achieve specific goals.* Here ritual action is used by participants as a means to a particular end or is judged by leaders on its ability to move the assembly toward a designated outcome. For example, a particular congregation could try to correlate growth in numbers to ways in which communion is celebrated.

5. *Through a commitment to justice.* Community leaders and participants identify particular justice issues and invite the community to work together toward a moral end. This position has been championed by recent feminist critiques of the abuse of liturgical authority by those who have sought to maintain the status quo. By excluding women from primary leadership roles, many ecclesial bodies have failed to recognize and affirm the gifts of all

the baptized. Only by opening the liturgical assembly to include voices of leaders from all who are baptized and gifted by the Spirit can justice be attained.

This fifth position that Grimes proposes invites assemblies to identify particular justice issues and through the lens of this perspective examine their current practices and theological presuppositions. This commitment to justice leads Grimes to advocate a posture of supinity, of an openness to the earth and all that surrounds us, which he refers to as "liturgical supinity." Grimes concludes: "Ritual has authority only insofar as it is rooted in, generated by, and answerable to its infrastructures—bodily, cultural, ecological, spiritual."[2] Grimes advocates that adopting a commitment to justice allows communities to critique abuses of authority inherent in other approaches. In light of this approach, we need to raise difficult questions about current practice if we want to reshape our rituals to reflect our commitment to social justice. For example, following the tragic events of 9/11, a congregation wrestled with the need to provide space that welcomed people for prayer and meditation. In the process, the leaders were forced to balance competing values: how do we maintain a sense of safety for ourselves and our buildings and at the same time unlock the church doors and welcome strangers?

Other questions need to be raised in regard to Grimes's analysis of the basis of our practices. For example, what is the ecological impact of the way that we gather as an assembly? This question could lead us to examine our consumption of resources, from printed orders of worship to disposable communion cups. Similarly, our purchasing choices for basic items for worship services (from bread and wine to paper) may carry significant ecological and financial consequences. To give but one example, our increasing need to print extensive orders of worship contributes to the waste of limited resources. As a first step, we can use recycled paper and place recycling bins in the narthexes of our churches. Beyond these initial steps, we can limit the amount of paper we use.

The primary purpose of investigating our own ritual practices is to ensure that our gatherings grow out of a commitment to work for justice in our relationships with one another and to preserve the earth. We cannot afford other appeals for the authority of our practices that ignore the primary need for assemblies of justice to gather around the table. People long for alternative communities where humans are welcomed and valued and invited into practices that work for social justice.

Incarnational Identity with Distinctive Features

Our work to create communities of justice is at the very center of an understanding of the church's role. Theologian Dietrich Bonhoeffer once wrote that the purpose of the church is to create physical space for the body of Christ in the world. "The answer of the New Testament is unambiguous. It holds that the church community claims a physical space here on earth not only for its worship and its order, but also for the daily life of its members."[3] The church itself becomes an incarnational sign that points to the presence of God in the world. Bonhoeffer suggests that this sign is present both in the church as a body as well as in individuals who live out of the vision of God's reign in our world. From this perspective, we gather as a congregation not to separate ourselves from the world, but to come together so that Christ's body is visibly present among us. Thus, the role of the church is to serve as an incarnational sign of God's promises to redeem us.

Gathering around the table each week is a primary way to make space for Christ in our assemblies. In the process, we discover that we are being made into the body of Christ as well. As we live out the vision of this new perspective, we carry the presence of Christ into the world even as we encounter it in the presence of our neighbors each day.

While churches share a common goal to be incarnational signs, congregations do not all look, sound, and act alike. This diversity can be a healthy sign of different ways of expressing Christian faith and life as it points to various ways in which God is present in our world. The accounts of the diverse ways of celebrating communion from the early church suggest that the future of the church is not a monolithic, prescribed liturgy. Instead, the shape of the table prayer provides a common framework that invites presiders and assemblies to express thanks in various ways. Song, dance, movement, language, artistic expression, and other ways of embodying the table prayer add local flavor to the assembly's worship.

What does the liturgy look and feel like in your congregation? Many church leaders continue to talk about the importance of enculturation in worship, of making room for local adaptation and expression. I remain convinced that the *need* for enculturation *requires* further exploration that delves deep below the surface issues. It is not enough simply to permit individual congregations to make adaptations as long as the structure of the service remains intact. Often, matters of enculturation revolve largely around forms of musical expression.[4] Instead of simply changing musical preferences and genres, we need a more robust dialogue about worship practices, one in which local models and patterns are held up as faithful and distinctive.

Table as Recipe

As congregations experience change and seek faithful options, they discover an abundance of alternative visions for the future of the church. A market-driven industry constantly provides programs that promise to provide rapid growth and success. Amid a preponderance of remedies, some congregations look at past worship patterns as ways to bring renewal. The successful growth of congregations during the 1950s prompts some Protestants to hold tight to historic twentieth-century worship patterns, which give priority to proclamation with relatively minimal attention to the sacraments. As a result, some recent forms of church architecture depict the sanctuary as a convention center. Religious symbols are diminished or removed. Liturgical furnishings are minimized. The pulpit takes on the characteristics of a stage, or the set for a television program, so that the preacher can bring us the news of the day. Contemporary services with a heavy focus on musical expression in a popular cultural vein remain prevalent. In a similar form of retrenchment, a recent Roman Catholic announcement authorizing the use of the Latin mass in certain parishes suggests a retrenchment from the values of Vatican II with its newfound emphasis on the role of the assembly.

More recently, the language of the emergent church, especially with an interest in reclaiming ancient practices, has been adopted by growing number of congregations. While there seems to be little consensus about what emergent worship means or even looks like, the movement has provided space and energy for important conversations and experiments about recovering ancient elements of worship and placing them in new contexts. Emergent services often incorporate ritual elements such as incense and icons, which appeal to the senses, while relying on modern technology and wide varieties of musical expression.

In the midst of this search for worship renewal, I am advocating that congregations maintain a central focus on Scripture, table, and font. The table at the center of the assembly's gathering serves as an invitation to all who come. Gathering around the table to break bread and share the cup each Lord's Day is a defining practice of Christian assemblies regardless of time and place. With a faithful and rich prayer of thanksgiving and an open sharing of the elements, the congregation itself grows into the pattern of Christ's life, death, and resurrection. Sunday after Sunday, those who gather around the table learn the language and practice of table fellowship and the discipline of Christian formation. When leaders of the assembly model these patterns and members extend them into our shared daily lives, then congregations will become vibrant in their faith and life.

Becoming the Body of Christ

Recently I visited a small congregation that during the previous year had decided to adopt a service of Word and Table at each Sunday's gathering. In some ways, there is nothing particularly remarkable about this church. There was no PowerPoint projector or professional choir. I found myself deeply moved by simple things: the reading of Scripture, a brief and provocative sermon applying themes in the text to our lives, and a time of prayer in which the congregation praised God and called out for God's blessings on the needs of our world. The prayer at the table underscored God's creative work in the world, Christ's redemptive pattern, and the Spirit's movement within us toward wholeness. Then we gathered around the table to share in this bread and this wine in order that we might be signs of God's grace in our world. At the close of the service, congregational members stood up and invited us to join them during the week in attending a Bible study, serving in a soup kitchen, cleaning up the neighborhood school, and collecting blankets to give to homeless people before winter arrived. These acts of hope, hospitality, and service that begin in the Christian assembly and extend into the world are witnesses to Christian faith that is alive and vibrant.

In the end, recovering and practicing a full, embodied prayer that welcomes us to the table and sends us into the world prepares us for Christian life and service. Through our engagement with the Word, the experience of our baptismal journey, and the sustenance at the table, we are shaped and molded into the body of Christ. In his letter to the church at Rome, the apostle Paul writes about the ongoing process of sanctification as one grows and lives into the Christian life. Recent work on baptismal formation is beginning to *recover* practices that undergird the baptismal journey. Christian faith is not static but consists of the act of maturing in our discipleship. Baptismal formation is not accomplished at any one given time but is extended throughout one's life. By God's grace we are prepared for our baptism. In baptism we experience and claim our identity as followers of Jesus Christ and children of God. Through the Spirit's work we grow in faith to display signs of Christ's claim upon our lives.

Similarly, regularly gathering around the table to participate in communion provides a template for Christian virtues and practices: living with thankful hearts, forgiving our neighbors, depending on God's provision, welcoming strangers, practicing hospitality, sharing our belongings, recognizing Christ's presence, caring for all of God's creation, and giving up power.

In the end, this vision of congregational life that is grounded in worship renewal draws on the admonition to the church in Colossae. There the author encourages the community to make room for the Spirit to bring gifts for the upbuilding of the community:

"Clothe yourselves with compassion, kindness, humility, meekness, and patience" (Col. 3:12). Wrapped up, clothed, in these virtues, Christians grow into the image of Jesus Christ. Acts of charity and love hold us together in harmony and serve as a sign of peace to those around us. When we gather around the table, we practice these virtues. When we break bread with those with whom we disagree, then our differences are set aside in light of this common table practice that we share. When the cup is passed for all to share, our tendency to think primarily of our own needs is challenged. In this way, eating and drinking together at the table create a community grounded in the language of thanksgiving. When thanksgiving becomes the primary focus of our lives, then the prayer in Colossians becomes our own: "And whatever you do, in word or deed, do everything in the name of the Lord Jesus, giving thanks to God" (Col. 3:17).

Hymn for Reflection

As we gather at your Table,
as we listen to your Word,
help us know, O God, your presence;
let our hearts and minds be stirred.
Nourish us with sacred story
till we claim it as our own;
teach us through this holy banquet
how to make Love's victory known.

Turn our worship into witness
in the sacrament of life;
send us forth to love and serve you,
bringing peace where there is strife.
Give us Christ, your great compassion
to forgive as you forgave;
may we still behold your image
in the world you died to save.

Gracious Spirit, help us summon
other guests to share that feast
where triumphant Love will welcome
those who had been last and least.
There no more will envy blind us
nor will pride our peace destroy,
as we join with saints and angels
to repeat the sounding joy.[5]

Questions for Discussion

1. "Take," "bless," "break," and "give" are described as generous terms in the context of communion. Give examples from daily life and ministry in which these are words of generosity toward others. How do these actions call us "away from the selfish patterns of greed, consumption, self-absorption, and conceit" (page 123)?

2. On an eraser board, chalkboard, or paper, sketch your sanctuary, the shape of the room and its contents. Where are the Bible, table, and font? Talk about what happens in the sanctuary, especially with the sacraments, in light of what you have read in this book. Erase the walls of your sanctuary. How can what happens in the sanctuary be loosed into the world? What would this experience be like? How would it affect the world—and how would it affect you?

3. After a long period of time it is not uncommon to think about any action, "We've always done it this way." Discuss your table practice as your congregation currently experiences it. Then describe other ways you have experienced it in other churches, the various ways you have shared in communion. Are there any alternatives you would like to experiment with in your congregation?

4. Recite or sing together the Hymn for Reflection on pages 130–131. How are we nourished, fed, by the gospel? What does the Lord's Supper, "the holy banquet," teach us? If a visitor, a stranger, or a non-Christian witnessed your worship, what would that person see? What would he or she learn of what you believe?

Notes

Chapter 1, Coming to the Table

1. *Baptism, Eucharist and Ministry;* Faith and Order Paper No. 111, the "Lima Text" (Geneva, Switzerland: World Council of Churches, 1982).
2. "The First Apology of Justin Martyr," in Bard Thompson, *Liturgies of the Western Church* (New York: World Publishing, 1961), 9.
3. Ibid., 9.
4. *Book of Common Worship* (Louisville: Westminster John Knox, 1993), 156.
5. Fred Kaan, "Down to Earth, as a Dove"; hymn text copyright © 1968 by Hope Publishing Company, Carol Stream, IL 60188. All rights reserved. Used by permission.

Chapter 2, Gathering around the Table

1. I am indebted to my friend Cláudio Carvalhaes for this example.
2. "To complete the picture, although the evidence is more limited, there are also some signs that in certain communities other foodstuffs may have accompanied the bread and water (or wine) at the ritual meals and a thanksgiving said over them. Thus oil along with bread, vegetables, and salt appears in one of the eucharistic meals in the Acts of Thomas; and salt also features in the Pseudo-Clementine Homilies. Furthermore, milk and honey form

part of the baptismal Eucharist in several ancient sources; and oil, cheese and olives are provided with prayers in the Apostolic Tradition. Both of these may be the remains of eucharistic traditions that once regularly included a wider range of food . . ." Paul Bradshaw, *Eucharistic Origins* (Oxford: Oxford University Press, 2004), 59.

3. It is worth noting that there has been recent change in some communities in this regard: both bread and cup (and not just communion in one kind) are shared, and others use a loaf of bread instead of communion wafers.

4. *Book of Common Worship*, Easter Prayer, 321.

5. Marty Haugen, "Gather Us In"; hymn text copyright © 1983 by GIA Publications, Inc., 7404 S. Mason Ave., Chicago, IL 60638 (800-442-1358; www.giamusic.com). All rights reserved. Used by permission.

Chapter 3, Re-membering the Body of Christ

1. *Evangelical Lutheran Worship* (Minneapolis: Augsburg Fortress, 2006), 307. The prayer is part of Morning Prayer and especially recommended for Sundays.

2. *Book of Common Worship*, 921.

3. It is worth noting that the context of these words themselves is highly contested. In 1 Corinthians, Jesus's words are not located in the setting of a Passover meal. In the Gospel of Luke, the words are part of a variant reading of the text. In Matthew and Mark, they are absent from the Last Supper narrative altogether.

4. Laurence Stookey, *Eucharist: Christ's Feast with the Church* (Nashville: Abingdon, 1993), 28.

5. I was stunned by this nuance when I heard these words at a communion celebration in the chapel at Emory University.

6. Jerome offers this interpretation in his later commentary on the Gospel of John. Raymond Brown (among other scholars) offers it as one possible interpretation of the text in *The Gospel According to John, XIII–XXI, The Anchor Bible*, vol. 29A (Garden City, N.Y.: Doubleday, 1970), 1074.

7. In his classic work *The Shape of the Liturgy* (Westminster [London], U.K.: Dacre, 1945), Dom Gregory Dix recognized this sequence of actions as constitutive and foundational for identifying the shape of the liturgy itself.

8. *The Liturgy of John Knox* (Glasgow: University Press, 1886), 145–46.

9. Jeffrey Rowthorn, "At the Font We Start Our Journey"; hymn text copyright © 1991 by Hope Publishing Company, Carol Stream, IL 60188. All rights reserved. Used by permission.

Chapter 4, Welcoming Friend and Stranger

1. Brian Wren, "I Come with Joy," copyright © 1971; revised hymn text copyright © 1995 Hope Publishing Company, Carol Stream, IL 60188. All rights reserved. Used by permission.

2. Some interpreters also understand the reference to the five loaves as a metaphor for the five books of the Law.

3. Mark's Gospel underscores the significance of these numbers by adding Jesus's discourse to the disciples about the importance of these numbers in Mark 8:14-21.

4. From a presentation by Alan Roxburgh, church leader and consultant.

5. Ruth 2:4.

6. See the helpful discussion of this matter in Ron Byars, *Lift Your Hearts on High: Eucharistic Prayer in the Reformed Tradition* (Louisville: Westminster John Knox, 2004), 27. Byars notes the important theological place these words held in Calvin's theology in the debate over Christ's presence. Byars also offers insights into the present metaphorical meaning of these words.

7. Wren, "I Come with Joy."

Chapter 5, Discovering God and Finding Our Own Identity

1. *Celebrate God's Presence: A Book of Services for The United Church of Canada* (Etobicoke, Ontario: The United Church Publishing House, 2000), 275.

2. These words include references to a prayer adapted from the Alexandrine Liturgy of St. Basil that can be found in the *Book of Common Worship*, 146.

3. Philip Newell, Altar Garden Liturgy for St. John's House, Portsmouth, England, unpublished.

4. These examples are drawn from communion prayers in *Celebrate God's Presence: A Book of Services for the United Church of Canada*. See particularly communion prayers B and F. Prayer B includes the option to add other biblical figures from readings for the day.

5. Ibid., Prayer B, 243. Some recent Eucharistic prayers are careful to name both women and men as biblical models.

6. Gail Ramshaw, "The Long and Short of Eucharistic Praying," *Call to Worship: Liturgy, Music, Preaching and the Arts*, vol. 40. 4:36. The next section of the prayer models a similar pattern with Mary Magdalene, Peter, and Paul as witnesses of faithful Christians with room for other names to be added.

7. Here the communion prayer prefigures themes of self-offering that are highlighted in the next section of the prayer that gives thanks for Jesus's life and witness.

8. Frank C. Senn, *Christian Liturgy: Catholic and Evangelical* (Minneapolis: Fortress, 1997), 85.

9. Fred Pratt Green, "For the Fruit of All Creation"; hymn text copyright © 1970 by Hope Publishing Company, Carol Stream, IL 60188. All rights reserved. Used by permission.

Chapter 6, Encountering Christ and Offering Ourselves

1. Romans 12:1. The NRSV uses "reasonable" as the variant reading for "spiritual" service. In this chapter, I will highlight the significance of communion as a way of offering our whole selves in thanksgiving to God.

2. Roman Catholic biblical scholars like Raymond Brown have been particularly helpful in helping identify ways that sacraments may be referenced throughout the Gospels.

3. For a helpful discussion of the variety of biblical and theological models of atonement, see Paul Fiddes, *Past Event and Pres-*

ent Salvation: The Christian Idea of Atonement (London: Dayton, Longman & Todd, Ltd.), 1989.

4. *Book of Common Worship*, 201.

5. The catechumenate as a model of baptismal preparation is particularly helpful with its emphasis on a time of discernment following baptism that invites new Christians to explore and identify their gifts and opportunities for service.

6. Ron Byars offers this suggestion in *Lift Your Hearts on High: Eucharistic Prayer in the Reformed Tradition* (Louisville: Westminster John Knox, 2005), 29. He offers this perspective as a sharp contrast to the medieval understanding of the mass as Christ's sacrifice.

7. It is worth noting that this perspective grew out of the Reformed tradition, where the communion prayer has often carried a penitential nature. If we are seeking to recover the practice of a joyful feast, it is difficult for me to see how this is a sacrificial act on the part of the congregation.

8. Following Augustine, Calvin often referred to the sacraments as "visible words."

9. Oscar Romero; see www.creighton.edu/CollaborativeMinistry/romero.html.

10. From a service at Union (N.Y.) seminary, Cláudio Carvalhaes presiding.

11. Worship leaders must show caution in planning these services so that the Lord's Supper is not used to manipulate a church group to hold together. Instead, the table can serve as a starting point for lively and animated discussion that may not lead to agreement, but does not lead to a point of rupture.

12. *Iona Abbey Worship Book* (Glasgow: Wild Goose Publications, 2001), 113–14.

13. Some scholars argue that the Words of Institution were added extemporaneously, but no documents support this claim. It is also interesting to note a recent decision by the Vatican to recognize the eucharistic prayer of the Assyrian Church of the East, which does not use the Words of Institution in a "coherent narrative way . . . but rather in a dispersed euchological way, that is, integrated in successive prayers of thanksgiving, praise, and intercession." Cited in John F. Baldovin, S.J., "The Usefulness of

Liturgical History" (*Proceedings of the North American Academy of Liturgy*, 2007), 27. Baldovin goes on to note the astonishing nature of this claim in a tradition that has mandated exact words to include in the prayer at table.

14. Brian Gerrish's wonderful book *Grace and Gratitude: The Eucharistic Theology of John Calvin* (Minneapolis: Fortress Press, 1993) shows the significance of a full eucharistic theology in Calvin's work, yet Calvin's own table prayer remained quite sparse.

15. See Ron Byars, "Praying the Great Thanksgiving," *Call to Worship: Liturgy, Music, Preaching and the Arts,* vol. 40:4, 25–26.

16. For example, the *United Methodist Book of Worship* notes that during the Words of Institution: "The pastor may hold hands, palms down, over the bread [or cup], or touch the bread [or cup], or lift the bread [or cup]" (Nashville: United Methodist Publishing House, 1992), 37.

17. Philip H. Pfatteicher and Carlos R. Messerli, *Manual on the Liturgy: Lutheran Book of Worship* (Minneapolis: Augsburg, 1979), 239.

18. Byars, "Praying the Great Thanksgiving," 26.

19. Daniel L. Schutte, "Table of Plenty"; hymn text copyright © 1992 by Daniel L. Schutte. Published by OCP Publications, 4436 NE Hassalo, Portland, OR 97213. All rights reserved. Used with permission.

Chapter 7, Experiencing the Spirit and Naming the World before God

1. *Book of Common Prayer* (New York: Seabury, 1979), 375.

2. *Book of Common Worship.*

3. Philip Newell, *Celtic Benedictions: Morning and Night Prayer* (Grand Rapids: Eerdmans, 2000), 22. See also examples from the medieval Irish literature:

I am the wind which breathes upon the sea,
I am the wave of the ocean,
I am the murmur of the billows . . .

I am a beam of the sun . . .
I am a salmon in the water,
I am a lake in the plain,
I am a word of knowledge . . .
I am the God who created the fire in the head . . .

In James Mackey, *An Introduction to Celtic Christianity* (Edinburgh: T & T Clark Ltd, 1995), 78.

4. Thich Nhat Hanh, *Peace Is Every Step: The Path of Mindfulness in Everyday Life* (New York: Bantam Books, 1991), 22.

5. One of the eucharistic prayers from *Celebrate God's Presence* follows up on this Pauline language in its invocation of the Spirit: "Send, O God, your Holy Spirit upon us and upon these gifts, that all who share in this loaf and cup may be the body of Christ: light, life, and love in the world," 250.

6. Newell, *Celtic Benedictions*, 14.

7. *Book of Common Worship*, 72. The *United Methodist Book of Worship* uses the following words: "Make them be for us the body and blood of Christ, that we may be for the world the body of Christ," 38.

8. Prayer F in *Celebrate God's Presence*, 258.

9. I am grateful to Ron Byars for modeling this lesson in our seminary community.

10. Marty Haugen, "Spirit Blowing Through Creation"; hymn text copyright © 1987 by GIA Publications, Inc., 7404 S. Mason Ave., Chicago, IL 60638 (800-442-1358; www.giamusic.com). All rights reserved. Used by permission.

Chapter 8, Eating with Our Eyes Open

1. The Lord's Prayer, ecumenical version.

2. The recent English ecumenical version of the Lord's Prayer offers a way for a shared prayer by Christians of different traditions. See *Praying Together: A Revision of Prayers We Have in Common* (Nashville: Abingdon, 1988).

3. I often hear invitations to the table that suggest that we did not prepare this meal but that the Lord prepared it. While there is

certainly a sense that the risen Christ is present and calls us to the table, such language denies the obvious fact that people did prepare the table as part of their Christian discipleship. By speaking of Christ as host, we seek to give divine authority to the actions at the table.

4. For example, the call of Levi results in Jesus's eating in Levi's house. Similarly, the Zacchaeus narrative clearly declares that Jesus is the guest at table in his house. It strikes me that a pattern for leadership could be related to the earlier discussion of Matthew 25 in which disciples are distinguished by their willingness to discover Christ in those who are often forgotten or ignored.

5. This description comes from an e-mail exchange between Charles Hedley, the priest at St. James, and Ron Rienstra, a Reformed pastor. I am indebted to Chip Andrus, a Presbyterian pastor, and to Ron Rienstra for calling this practice to my attention.

6. Donald Reeves, *Down to Earth: A New Vision for the Church* (London: Mowbray, 1996).

7. Those who work in the theater and the arts can be important conversation partners in helping us analyze ritual patterns and practices in our worship spaces.

8. Sandro Carletti, *Guide to the Catacombs of Priscilla*, trans. Alice Mulhern (Vatican City: Pontifical Commission for Sacred Archaeology, 2005), 30–31.

9. Many scholars have noted similar themes in the wedding at Cana in John 2. The massive amounts of wine serve as an early sign of Jesus's ministry in John's Gospel.

10. From an interview done by Troy Lesher-Thomas.

11. John L. Bell and Graham Maule, "The Time Was Early Evening"; hymn text copyright © 1988 by GIA Publications, Inc., 7404 S. Mason Ave., Chicago, IL 60638 (800-442-1358; www.giamusic.com). All rights reserved. Used by permission.

Chapter 9, Eucharist as a Way of Life

1. It is worth noting that the language in the Presbyterian Church's *Directory for Worship* has been softened on this point.

y

Earlier claims that Jesus "instituted" the sacraments now suggest that Christ "commended" the sacraments.

2. Ronald Grimes, *Reading, Writing, and Ritualizing: Ritual in Fictive, Liturgical, and Public Places* (Washington: Pastoral Press, 1993), 56.

3. Dietrich Bonhoeffer, *Discipleship*, vol. 4, trans. John D. Godsey, *Dietrich Bonhoeffer Works* (Minneapolis: Fortress Press, 2003), 232.

4. The debates between advocates of "contemporary" and "traditional" services draw on distinctions between praise music and standard hymnody, often with little broader conversation about the basic substance and structure of the service. Similarly, enculturation is not simply about local rhythm instruments and attire. True enculturation is about taking the central things in worship (word, water, and table) and expressing them in ways that are authentic to the cultural context.

5. Carl P. Daw Jr., "As We Gather At Your Table"; hymn text copyright © 1989 by Hope Publishing Company, Carol Stream, IL 60188. All rights reserved. Used by permission.

Other Books in the Vital Worship, Healthy Congregations Series

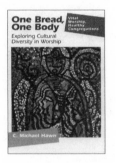

One Bread, One Body: Exploring Cultural Diversity in Worship by C. Michael Hawn

Designing Worship Together: Models and Strategies for Worship Planning by Norma deWaal Malefyt and Howard Vanderwell

When God Speaks through Change: Preaching in Times of Congregational Transition by Craig A. Satterlee

Where 20 or 30 Are Gathered: Leading Worship in the Small Church by Peter Bush and Christine O'Reilly

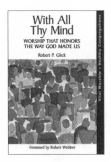

With All Thy Mind: Worship That Honors the Way God Made Us by Robert P. Glick

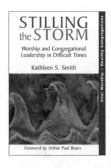

Stilling the Storm: Worship and Congregational Leadership in Difficult Times by Kathleen S. Smith

The Work of the People: What We Do in Worship and Why by Marlea Gilbert, Christopher Grundy, Eric T. Myers, and Stephanie Perdew

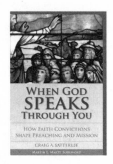

When God Speaks through You: How Faith Convictions Shape Preaching and Mission by Craig A. Satterlee

Preaching Ethically: Being True to the Gospel, Your Congregation, and Yourself by Ronald D. Sisk

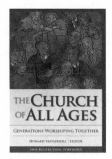

The Church of All Ages: Generations Worshiping Together edited by Howard Vanderwell

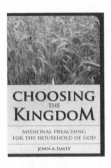

*Choosing the Kingdom:
Missional Preaching for the
Household of God* by John A.
Dally

Coming Soon

Worship Frames: How We Shape and Interpret Our Experience of God
by Deborah Kapp